Tigger
on the couch

The neuroses, psychoses, disorders
and maladies of our favourite
childhood characters

Laura James

Collins

Laura James is an author, journalist and magazine editor. Her writing appears in many national newspapers and magazines. She is also a consultant to cool hunters, The Next Big Thing. She lives in Norfolk and is married with four children. This is her sixth book.

First published in 2007 by Collins,
an imprint of
HarperCollins Publishers
77-85 Fulham Palace Road
London W6 8JB

www.collins.co.uk

11   10   09   08   07

5   4   3   2   1

Text © Laura James, 2007
Illustrations © Willie Ryan, 2007

Editorial Director: Jenny Heller
Assistant Editor: Kerenza Swift
Designer: Bob Vickers
Cover Design: Emma Ewbank

Mixed Sources
Product group from well-managed forests and other controlled sources
www.fsc.org Cert no. SW-COC-1806
© 1996 Forest Stewardship Council
FSC

ISBN 978-0-00-724895-7

Printed in Great Britain by William Clowes Ltd

This book is for all those bravely
battling a psychological disorder
and to the dedicated professionals
who work tirelessly to help them.

Contents

Foreword

Laura James has approached the concept of mental disorder from a different and very inventive direction. In doing so, I think she has made a valuable contribution to demystifying and destigmatising mental disorder. She has not set out to produce a psychiatric textbook but instead something that is accessible to a much broader audience.

Fairy tales – often the same stories differently told – are common across many cultures, and they serve a valuable role in helping children in particular to learn about and accept core values and attributes which they can aspire to emulate. Equally, fairy tales teach behaviour and values that children should seek to avoid – lessons that are not lost on adults either.

Children's stories also show how individuals with deficits and difficulties can still be valued, respected and well-liked members of the community, something which sadly society does not always remember, particularly where mental disorder is concerned. It is of note that in Laura's book the one character who has no mental disorder is Alice, about whose personality (rather than her exploits) we can remember very little. In life as in literature, it is the people with flaws and problems who we find interesting and they can teach us a lot.

This book does not set out to cover mental disorders in any encyclopaedic fashion, and because of the nature of children's stories and fairy tales, the emphasis is mainly on problems with personality rather than major mental illness. That is no bad thing, as the field of personality disorder and vulnerability is still neglected within the wider field of mental health. Many patients have a combination of personality vulnerabilities; in reality cases are often not as clear-cut as their fairy-tale counterparts, but then imaginary worlds are never meant to be mirror images of reality.

I have very much enjoyed working with Laura on this book, albeit my contribution has been minimal. I do hope that the readers of this book will enjoy the experience half as much as I have in helping Laura undertake this work: I have no doubt that all will find it both informative and entertaining.

Dr Gareth Vincenti MB, BS, LLB, FRCPsych
Consultant Psychiatrist and Medical Director
Cygnet Hospital Harrogate

Introduction

Once upon a time there was a little girl who loved to read. From the moment she discovered books, she was hooked and wanted more and more, until her bedroom contained so many that it resembled a library. Every night she'd climb into bed with a book and a torch, and travel to magical worlds of beautiful princesses, frog princes, wicked witches and talking animals who frolicked in forests.

Then she grew up and, having kissed rather a lot of frogs, finally got married and had children of her own. Out came our heroine's childhood books and she read to her babies until they begged her to stop. Then one evening, while reading *Cinderella* to her own little princesses, she realised that perhaps there was something she had missed. Did something rather less than magical lurk beneath the surface of the story that had passed quite unnoticed by her younger, more innocent self?

Should Cinderella have married a man she'd met only twice and was it healthy, she wondered, for Cinderella to have behaved in such a subservient fashion towards her stepsisters? Was she, perhaps, suffering from an underlying psychological disorder?

And was this in fact the case with other well-known and well-loved characters, too? Growing curiouser and curiouser, our heroine dug out an old copy of *Peter Pan* and flicked through the pages. The more she read, the more she realised that Neverland was indeed a dysfunctional community. And, so it went on, with Wonderland, Oz, the Hundred Acre Wood, and all the many magical places she had visited as a child. In almost every story someone was suffering.

Some found it impossible to control their tempers; others felt they must do anything to please those around them. Some found it very hard to concentrate; many suffered from deep depressions or low self-esteem. And then there were those who just wanted to go home.

As our heroine had a keen interest in psychology, she pondered what would happen if these characters were able to pick up the phone and arrange to see a therapist. Would their pain be alleviated? Would talking through their issues prove helpful or might drugs be required? On and on the questions went, until the voices in her head grew too loud to ignore and she started to jot down observations in her notebook.

Hour after hour she scribbled away, looking deep into the psyches of all her favourite fictional characters, from the Queen of Hearts to Winnie-the-Pooh. She spoke to doctors, psychiatrists and therapists. She trawled through textbooks seeking answers and decided, eventually, that something could, indeed should, be done. These poor creatures should not suffer in silence – help was out there.

Having spent a great deal of time in the self-help section of her local bookshop, however, she noticed that something appeared to be missing. Where were the books for princes who had been cursed, for inattentive bears or wolves needing to address their psychopathic tendencies? They weren't in the relationship section or on the self-improvement shelf. In fact, after trawling through the whole shop – which included, for some reason, a foray into cookery – she discovered no one had thought to write a book about the disorders of fictional characters.

This can't be right, she mused. How can a co-dependent girl, forced to live with a beast, cope if there's no book offering support and teaching her how to deal with her situation?

It was with this in mind that our heroine sought help in the traditional way. She got in touch with her very own fairy godmother, who happened to be an editor at one of the kindest, most beautiful publishers in all the land. Her opening line was perhaps an unusual one: 'I'm worried about Tigger,' she said, voice full of emotion. 'I think he has Attention Deficit Hyperactive Disorder and I'm sure he needs help.'

Her fairy godmother rose immediately to the challenge. Sadly, she didn't provide glass slippers on this occasion, which would have been nice, but she did wave her magic wand and said that, of course, all whimsical characters must have access to self-help literature, and a book exploring the problems experienced by our lovable friends must be published forthwith.

While it's sad to think of all these characters suffering for so long, it's heartening to know that help is at hand and that they just need to be pointed in the right direction. That's true for everyone, whether they're living in a land far, far away, or just around the corner. No one should suffer in silence, or feel ashamed about their problems. By writing this book, our heroine hoped that, as well as helping her fictional friends, it might give readers some insight into different psychological disorders and increase their awareness about those who might be suffering from one, even amongst their own acquaintance. Readers may well know of a 'people pleaser' like Cinderella or Wendy, for instance, or someone with narcissistic tendencies like the Queen of Hearts or the Wizard of Oz.

And that is the story of how *Tigger on the Couch* came to be. As in any fairy-tale quest, it was not without its villains – nasty deadlines crept up from dark corners and had to be fought – but, eventually, good won over evil and the book was written.

So, next time you curl up to read a bedtime story, perhaps you might consider the characters in a different light. Imagine, for example, Cruella de Vil, not ensconced at Hell Hall, but instead in the waiting room of a psychiatrist's office, box of tissues to hand and with a real determination to tackle her problems and become a valuable member of society.

With a little kindness, professional therapy and perhaps some psycho-pharmaceutical intervention, there's every possibility that many of our favourite characters will indeed live happily ever after.

The Pathologies in Wonderland

Many communities appear quite normal and it is only when one pokes beneath the surface one realises all is not as it seems.

In Wonderland, however, it is much more a case of what you see is what you get. As the Cheshire Cat rather crudely puts it, 'Everyone in Wonderland is mad.'

The very real point he's making is that most, indeed perhaps all, of Wonderland is actually suffering from some form of psychiatric illness.

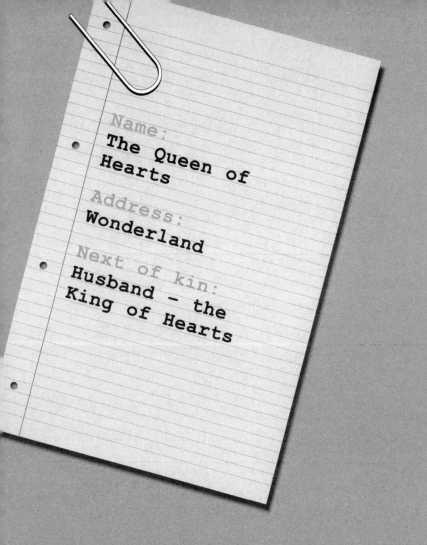

Name:
The Queen of Hearts

Address:
Wonderland

Next of kin:
Husband — the King of Hearts

'Off with her head!'

The Queen of Hearts

Diagnosis
Acquired Situational Narcissism
Power has gone to the Queen's head, causing her to feel superior.

Physical presentation
The Queen appears aloof, haughty and arrogant.

Diet
The Queen of Hearts is fond of tarts and Mock Turtle Soup. These are unlikely to aggravate her condition.

Family background
Nothing is known of the Queen's family of origin, except perhaps there were a pack of them.

Patient notes
The Queen of Hearts appears to rule Wonderland along with the King. The power inherent in her position has caused her to terrorise her subjects, behave with no empathy, and to act in a totally destructive way.

The Queen has a grandiose sense of self-worth and of entitlement, plus a tendency to exploit those around her. If she dislikes something that has been said or done, she has only one response: 'Off with his/her head!' Although in the case of the narcoleptic Dormouse, who once irritated her by talking in his sleep, she was more expansive in her fury: 'Behead that Dormouse! Turn that Dormouse out of court! Suppress him! Pinch him! Off with his whiskers!'

Such is the strength of the Queen's rages that the residents of Wonderland will go to extraordinary lengths to placate her – to the extent that her gardeners even painted the white roses red, knowing she preferred this colour. Predictably, when she caught them doing this she instantly ordered their execution.

The Queen shows a complete lack of empathy towards animals, and is often cruel to them. She uses flamingos as croquet mallets and hedgehogs as balls, for instance. On one occasion, she insisted the Mock Turtle should explain to Alice what Mock Turtle Soup is, showing no regard for how this might affect him. The Mock Turtle sobbed throughout the exchange, but the Queen had, by this point, moved on to tormenting someone else.

On a single day in Wonderland, she ordered at least 20 executions. The reasons for punishment were indiscriminate; they included bringing the cook tulip roots instead of onions – as one of the gardeners unwittingly did – and even 'murdering the time', of which the Hatter was accused.

The King, while capable of acts of kindness, actually encourages his wife's tyranny. Whenever he has to deal with anyone difficult, he uses to his own advantage her strategy for dealing with disappointment, namely calling in the executioner.

Great attention is paid to the Queen's every whim. When the Knave of Hearts was perhaps unjustifiably accused of stealing tarts the Queen had made, a trial ensued. Almost everyone in Wonderland was present and those who had no knowledge of the event were called as witnesses and intimidated into giving evidence against the Knave. Tellingly, there was an expectation that a sentence would be handed down even before a verdict was reached.

Acquired Situational Narcissism – the facts

While many traits are similar to Narcissistic Personality Disorder (see the Wizard of Oz, p. 100, for more information), which has its roots in childhood, Acquired Situational Narcissism occurs chiefly in individuals who become famous, such as a singer or film star, or who occupy a position of power, such as a politician or the head of a large company. It can also affect the super-rich.

Prognosis

Individuals with this disorder have particular difficulty adjusting to growing old and losing their former 'superiority'. Interpersonal relationships are often impaired due to problems derived from the individual's sense of entitlement, their need for admiration, and their disregard for the feelings of others. This can leave the person without support when significant relationships have broken down, which, in turn, can lead to depression. It is unlikely that those with this disorder would seek treatment. If they do, some improvement can be expected, however.

Treatment

While this disorder is exceptionally difficult to treat, psychotherapy can prove helpful in assisting the patient to look closely at their self-defeating behaviours. The therapist can help the patient achieve specific goals. In the Queen of Hearts' case, her sense of entitlement and complete disregard for the feelings of others require immediate attention. The Queen, notwithstanding her royal status, must learn to see everyone as her equal – or rather less *unequal*. This will be painful for her and it is unlikely she will stay the course of treatment. There is no medication available to treat this disorder, although if there are accompanying symptoms, such as depression, then medication may be considered as part of the treatment.

HAVE YOU COME ACROSS A QUEEN OF HEARTS?

Does someone you know suffer from delusions of grandeur? Has the person in question ...

achieved great fame? ☐

acquired great wealth or a position of power? ☐

lost their ability to empathise? ☐

come to behave in a grandiose and self-important fashion? ☐

come to behave in a way that could be described as destructive, outrageous or foolish? ☐

become excessively self-involved? ☐

displayed a need to be told how great they are? ☐

failed to observe social norms? ☐

appeared to believe they are omnipotent? ☐

surrounded themselves with 'yes men'? ☐

indulged in risk-taking behaviour? ☐

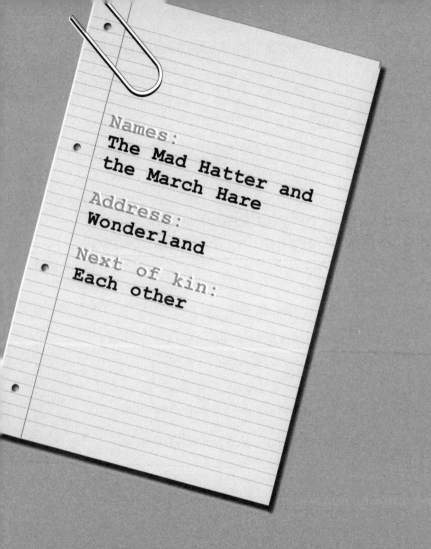

Names:
The Mad Hatter and the March Hare

Address:
Wonderland

Next of kin:
Each other

'Why is a raven like a writing desk?'

The Mad Hatter and the March Hare

Diagnosis
Shared Psychotic Disorder (*Folie à Deux*)
The March Hare and the Hatter share prominent delusions.

Physical presentation
The March Hare and the Mad Hatter appear healthy and well turned out, and seem to have no physical tics.

Diet
The Hatter and the March Hare eat only high tea.

Family background
Nothing is known of either of their families of origin.

Patient notes
The March Hare and the Mad Hatter have a close emotional bond. They spend much time together and share many delusional beliefs. This significantly impairs their social functioning.

For example, at a tea party hosted by the March Hare, he and the Hatter were reported to cry, 'No room! No room!'

to Alice, when there were clearly plenty of spare places laid. Later it transpired that they believe it is always six o'clock and therefore always teatime – and thus they must always be having tea. This causes significant difficulty in their day-to-day lives, such as maintaining basic housekeeping. As the Hatter explained to Alice: 'It is always teatime, and we've no time to wash the things between whiles.'

They find creative, if disordered, ways to deal with such problems. Instead of washing up, they simply set a large number of places and move around when the cups and plates become dirty.

Like the Queen of Hearts, the Hatter and the March Hare find the Dormouse's narcolepsy irritating. They attempt to deal with it by dunking the Dormouse in a teapot or spilling tea on his whiskers, acts which further illustrate their inability to deal with problems in a healthy way.

At the tea party, the March Hare offered wine to Alice when there was none, as if this were normal practice. The Hatter asked her nonsensical questions for which there could be no rational answers, such as: 'Why is a raven like a writing desk?' As is the case with the March Hare and the Mad Hatter, sufferers of a shared psychosis are, in the main, oblivious to each other's eccentricities.

The March Hare and Hatter undertake projects together which fail because of their lack of logic or forethought. For example, they tried to fix the March Hare's broken watch with butter. Rather than realising they had made a mistake, they blamed one another for the failure. The Hatter declared: 'I told you butter wouldn't suit the works!' To which the March Hare offered the explanation: 'It was the *best* butter' as if the quality of the butter would have somehow made it more likely to succeed.

Most of their shared delusions relate to time. It would be fascinating to know if their delusion is such that they believe time could change in this way for everyone or if time is personal.

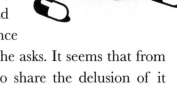

While most of their delusions are shared, on occasion the Hatter acknowledges the March Hare's insanity. He talks, for example, about the March Hare going mad one March day and says that, since then, the Hare won't do a thing he asks. It seems that from this moment they both began to share the delusion of it always being six o'clock.

Shared Psychotic Disorder – the facts

This is a highly unusual disorder, characterised by two people in a close emotional relationship sharing the same or similar delusions. There is usually a primary case, namely the individual who had delusions first, and a secondary case – the other half of the pair, who takes on the primary case's delusional beliefs. Although it is most common for two people to suffer from this disorder, it is possible for larger groups or even families to experience a shared psychosis.

Prognosis

Without intervention, a shared disorder is unlikely to improve. The delusions will endure and it is possible new beliefs will appear. Separation can provoke an improvement in the less disordered individual, who may see the delusions disappear. However, in the case of the Hatter and the March Hare, it is difficult to know which one this might be. Because this disorder usually occurs in long-standing relationships, the individuals generally resist separation and fear change.

Treatment

Once separated, each sufferer would usually undergo a course of psychotherapy. Inpatient treatment can be useful, as it allows each to be treated individually. Antipsychotic drugs would also usually be prescribed.

HOW TO IDENTIFY A CASE OF FOLIE À DEUX

If one or more of these applies, seek medical advice:

Is the person you are concerned about in a relationship with someone who previously had delusional beliefs? ☐

Does the person take either prescription medications or have a history of substance abuse? ☐

Have they been screened for other disorders such as schizophrenia? ☐

Have they been checked for other medical conditions? ☐

Is the new sufferer's delusion similar to that of the original sufferer? ☐

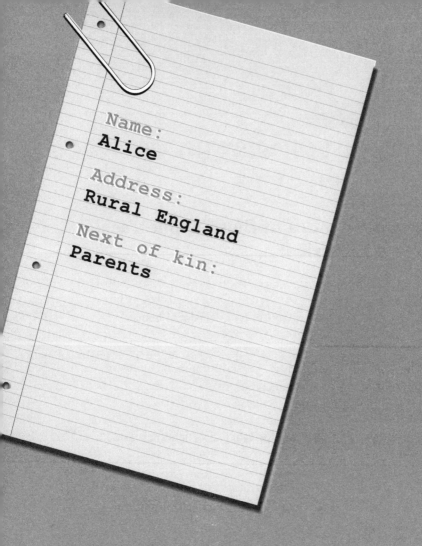

Name:
Alice

Address:
Rural England

Next of kin:
Parents

'But I don't want to go among mad people.'

Alice

Diagnosis
No disorder

Alice is a well-adjusted person who has found herself among a group of highly dysfunctional individuals.

Physical presentation
Alice appears healthy; there is no evidence of disability.

Diet
There is no indication that Alice eats anything out of the ordinary while at home. However, in Wonderland she has consumed a series of unusual foods that appear to have had a mind-altering effect, as well as changing her physical size. It would be advisable for her to avoid all foodstuffs and drink only water while in Wonderland.

Family background
Evidence suggests Alice's family function normally. She has an affectionate relationship with her older sister, who keeps a watchful eye over Alice and reminds her to go in for tea, and she is close enough to her brother to be aware of the details of his Latin prep.

Patient notes

Alice's early life appears to have been unremarkable. Her family seem well adjusted and there is no evidence to suggest any kind of abuse or neglect. They seem to get on well with each other and appear supportive.

Alice's intelligence level and social skills are age-appropriate. Her stable background, self-confidence and firm boundaries allow her to cope well in a most challenging and unusual situation. Her desire to follow the White Rabbit down the rabbit hole demonstrates normal childhood curiosity, with perhaps some impulsivity, displayed by her failure to consider the consequences of her actions as she plunged headlong after the rabbit. This is still within 'normal' parameters for her age, however.

While in Wonderland, Alice has met a series of disordered individuals. She has ingested substances that have changed her perceptions and altered her physical self. However, she has managed to keep calm in the face of adversity; to check that her faculties are all still intact, she will try some mental arithmetic, for example, or recite poems she has learned at school.

She displays healthy signs of optimism, too, and looks for the positive in every situation. As she tumbled down the rabbit hole, she reasoned it would make falling down the stairs at home less alarming.

Alice shows a proper sense of compassion and responsibility. She worries about who will feed her cat at home while she is in Wonderland. And despite its growing resemblance to a pig, she felt she should rescue the Duchess's baby for fear that, if it was left at home, it would be killed by the Duchess or her cook.

Alice's psychological boundaries remain firm despite the dysfunctional environment. For instance, she told the Hatter he shouldn't make personal remarks when he insulted her about her appearance, and she declared: 'Stuff and nonsense!' in response to the Queen's demand that she be beheaded.

When Alice is reduced to tears by her circumstances, she successfully self-soothes, saying that she must 'pull herself together'. And when called as a witness in the trial of the Knave of Hearts, she firmly maintained she knew nothing of the matter, despite intimidation from the judge. Having a strong sense of morality, she also insisted there must be a verdict before a defendant could be sentenced.

Prognosis

As Alice has coped well in Wonderland, there is no reason to assume that she will not continue to enjoy good mental health. However, she has had some unusual, frightening and difficult experiences, so it would be appropriate for her to be monitored to ensure she is not developing Post-traumatic Stress Disorder. Of course, it is important for Alice's family to acknowledge that she has been through an ordeal and to allow her to talk about it if she wishes. It may be difficult for her to come to terms with her experiences in Wonderland if she finds she is disbelieved by those around her.

Treatment

No treatment is required.

ARE YOU COMPLETELY NORMAL?

Answer these questions to see if you, like Alice, can keep your head while all those around you are losing theirs:

Are you able to stay calm in most circumstances? ☐

Do you find it easy to adapt to different social situations? ☐

Have you learned to take the rough with the smooth? ☐

Do you have firm personal boundaries that you can assert when needed? ☐

Can you maintain your core values in the face of opposition and keep to your own moral code? ☐

33

Wonderland on the couch

While the Queen of Hearts, the March Hare and the Mad Hatter have perhaps the most significant disorders in Wonderland, many others are suffering too.

Firstly, the social infrastructure in Wonderland is woefully inadequate. There appear to be no laws protecting children, animals or the vulnerable, and the whole judicial system is disordered and unfair, to say the least.

No agencies exist to help with parenting, emotional distress or substance abuse. Town planning is poor, with much of Wonderland unavailable to its residents due to accessibility issues, while newcomers can be too large to fit into the buildings, whether public or private, having to resort to extreme measures to reduce their size.

The Duchess has a violent disorder and is clearly an unfit mother. She shakes her baby, sings inappropriate songs and recommends children should be beaten simply for sneezing, suggesting they do it to tease their parents. She also throws her baby across the room and leaves it with Alice – a total stranger – so she can pursue her hobbies, notably playing croquet with the Queen.

The Dormouse suffers from narcolepsy, a disorder characterised by excessive daytime sleepiness. This strongly impairs his ability to function normally. Sadly, there is little sympathy for him in Wonderland, where political incorrectness runs amok, and he is often verbally or physically abused because of his disability.

There is strong evidence of substance abuse throughout Wonderland. The Caterpillar smokes a hookah and eats mushrooms that bring about an altered state. He encouraged Alice to also try the mushrooms, gaining her confidence initially by his authoritative air.

The White Rabbit's highly animated state clearly indicates an anxiety disorder. While he works hard to keep the peace and behave correctly, his nervous personality makes Wonderland a particularly unhealthy place for him. He needs order, structure and to know he is following the rules. The chaotic nature of his environment increases his feelings of anxiety, causing his movements to become twitchy and his general sense of unease to be magnified. He constantly repeats the phrase 'Oh my fur and whiskers!', which may suggest he also suffers from Obsessive–Compulsive Disorder.

The cook is oppositional, violent and deluded. She insists that the staple ingredient for any dish (including tarts) is pepper and sets out to induce sneezing fits in all she meets by terrorising them with a pepper mill. When displeased, she throws kitchen equipment at those close by and shows no restraint, even when there are children present. It is likely she will cause serious injury, perhaps even death, to an unfortunate bystander.

Without changes in the law, a regeneration programme and appropriate services being made available, it is difficult to see how things in Wonderland could be improved and life for its inhabitants made more bearable.

The Pathologies in Hundred Acre Wood

If you go out in the Wood today, you're sure of a big surprise. Far from the peaceful rural idyll that one might expect, the residents there are suffering from an array of troublesome symptoms, but which – with the correct treatment – could be easily alleviated.

It's interesting to note that many members of the community suffer from some form of psychological disorder, which must surely put Hundred Acre Wood near the top of the league table for neighbourhoods with mental health problems.

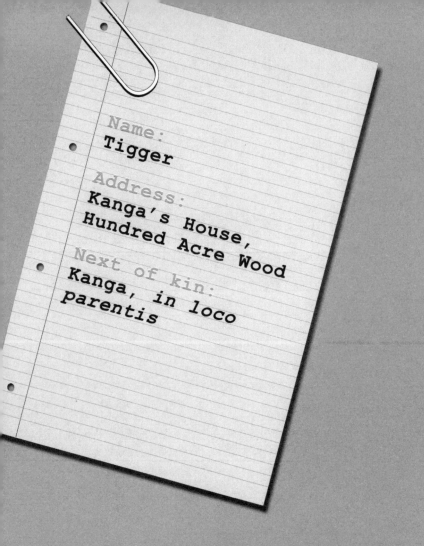

Name:
Tigger

Address:
**Kanga's House,
Hundred Acre Wood**

Next of kin:
**Kanga, in loco
parentis**

Perhaps Ritalin
is what Tigger
should like best.

Tigger

Diagnosis
Attention Deficit/Hyperactive Disorder (AD/HD), Predominantly Hyperactive –Impulsive Type

Tigger's continual bouncing, hyperactivity and irresponsible attitude cause problems for him and those with whom he lives, as well as those with whom he interacts in the wider community.

Physical presentation
Tigger rarely sits still. He's always running, climbing, bouncing or fidgeting.

Diet
Having tried – and firmly rejected – honey, haycorns and thistles, Tigger settles on extract of malt as his food of choice. While this particular substance is unlikely to exacerbate his condition, a more balanced diet (see p. 44) would almost certainly benefit him and perhaps contribute to an improvement in his behaviour.

Family background
No information is available on Tigger's life before his arrival at Pooh's house. Nothing is known of his previous address

or his family of origin, although it has been said that he is the only Tigger.

Tigger's arrival at Pooh's house in the middle of the night is evidence of his inability to control his impulses. A less disordered individual would have known that it is more appropriate to visit people during the day, especially when dropping in on someone one scarcely knows or has never met.

Impulsive behaviours, interrupting and intruding are at the heart of Tigger's problems. Soon after their first meeting, for example, Tigger suddenly interrupted Pooh, climbed on to the table, wrapped himself in his host's tablecloth and brought everything crashing to the floor. When questioned by Pooh about his behaviour, rather than accepting responsibility for his actions Tigger instead accused the tablecloth of trying to bite him.

Tigger makes bold statements, such as declaring that he is only bouncy before breakfast. He impulsively proclaims that whatever food he is offered is what Tiggers like best, then gulps down large mouthfuls of the food in question, only to find he dislikes it very much.

More evidence of Tigger's recklessness and poor impulse control is displayed by his belief that he can do anything. He has no sense of fear or responsibility. This was apparent when he climbed up a very high tree with Roo on his back before he had ascertained whether he was able to climb a tree in the first place. Inevitably, they then got stuck when he realised he had no idea of how to get down.

On one occasion, Tigger grabbed Roo's medicine from Kanga (with whom he currently lives, and who acts as a mother figure to him), which he proceeded to swallow, almost devouring the spoon as well. Obviously the medicine might have proved dangerous to him. Tigger never learns from his mishaps, bouncing back (all too literally as well as figuratively) almost immediately after a frightening and potentially hazardous incident has occurred. As a result, Tigger's behaviour causes concern and irritation to those around him.

Living with someone suffering from AD/HD can be very trying. Perhaps this is why Rabbit suggested the rather extreme measure of taking Tigger into the forest and losing him in the mist. Rabbit and his friends believed the shock of being lost might cause Tigger to calm down a little on his return, a strategy that backfired, however, when it became apparent that never getting lost was actually no hollow boast on Tigger's part. But this is very much the exception to prove the rule.

AD/HD – the facts

Attention Deficit/Hyperactivity Disorder is characterised by a persistent pattern of inattention and/or hyperactivity and impulsivity. There are three subtypes of this disorder. The first is AD/HD, Combined Type. Patients diagnosed with this form of AD/HD display both inattentive and hyperactive–impulsive symptoms, hence they'll behave as if they're Winnie-the-Pooh and Tigger rolled into one. They'll be dreamy and fail to finish tasks, as well as being fidgety and always on the go. The second type is the one Tigger meets the diagnostic criteria for – AD/HD, Predominantly Hyperactive–Impulsive Type. The third type is AD/HD, Predominantly Inattentive Type, for which Pooh meets the diagnostic criteria (see p. 49).

Predominantly Hyperactive–Impulsive Type

The subtype Predominantly Hyperactive–Impulsive is used when six or more symptoms of hyperactivity/impulsivity are present, but fewer than six symptoms of inattention. To be diagnosed with this version of AD/HD, the patient must have displayed symptoms before the age of seven and their behaviour must interfere with social, academic or occupational functioning. Hyperactivity is characterised by fidgeting (or, indeed, bouncing), running about or climbing in situations where such activity is inappropriate. It would appear to be impossible for sufferers to sit still. Impulsive behaviour includes interrupting someone while they are still speaking, undertaking activities that are likely to result in injury, and generally not considering the consequences of one's actions.

Prognosis

AD/HD is generally regarded as an incurable disorder. However, there are a number of effective treatments that would almost certainly help Tigger control his self-defeating behaviours.

Treatment

AD/HD is treated using a variety of approaches. Behaviour management at home and school is very important for a child (or a Tigger) with this disorder. Clear rules need to be set out. A psychiatrist or therapist will often help parents learn how to manage their child's behaviour. It would be a good idea for Kanga to attend some therapy sessions, as it is she who is  mainly in charge of caring for Tigger. Possibly family therapy could be considered, with Roo – an all-too-frequent 'partner in crime' – in attendance too. (For further comment on Roo's psychological profile, see 'Hundred Acre Wood on the couch' p. 66.)

Psychotherapy and behaviour therapy can be very helpful in teaching the child how to cope with the condition and learn to curb impulsive behaviour. Tigger could, for example, come to see how stepping back and considering his options could lead him to fulfilling forms of occupation that do not involve putting himself or others in any kind of danger.

Medication is sometimes prescribed. This tends to be a psychostimulant (such as Ritalin), which works by increasing the patient's attention span and reducing hyperactivity and impulsivity. When Roo takes his medicine, Tigger could be given his medication at the same time in order to allay any embarrassment he may feel at being treated for a psychological disorder.

Much success has also been reported by trying changes in the child's diet, such as cutting out foods containing artificial colouring and flavouring, and introducing substances that are high in omega-3 fatty acids. It may be discovered that Tiggers like oily fish, for instance.

As AD/HD is usually a lifelong condition, there are many adults who suffer from it too. However, with the correct treatment, the condition can be managed, so it has little impact on the sufferer's work life or relationships. Hopefully Tigger, following appropriate treatment and lifestyle adjustments, will emerge into adulthood an altogether calmer individual.

HOW TO IDENTIFY SOMEONE WITH AD/HD

Do you know a Tigger type? Do they ...

continually get up out of their seat when they should remain seated? ☐

find it seemingly impossible to keep their hands or feet still? ☐

find it hard to sit quietly or get on with something without making a fuss? ☐

run and climb about when such behaviour isn't expected, or (in older people) experience feelings of restlessness? ☐

gabble away inconsequentially? ☐

appear to be always on the go? ☐

find queuing or waiting difficult? ☐

interrupt or blurt things out? ☐

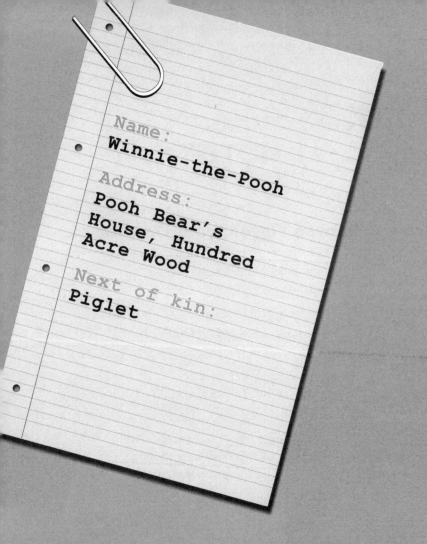

Name:
Winnie-the-Pooh
Address:
**Pooh Bear's
House, Hundred
Acre Wood**
Next of kin:
Piglet

Pooh's possible
honey addiction is
perhaps the least
of his problems.

Winnie-the-Pooh

Diagnosis
Attention Deficit/Hyperactive Disorder, Predominantly Inattentive Type

Winnie-the-Pooh's failure to pay attention to detail and his inability to think things through cause trouble in his day-to-day life.

Physical presentation
Pooh is extremely overweight, perhaps even clinically obese.

Diet
Pooh's diet consists mainly of honey. Much of his attention is taken up by food – either eating, procuring or counting it, and even just thinking about it.

Family background
No information is available on Pooh's early years or his family of origin.

Patient notes
Winnie-the-Pooh appears vague much of the time and often begins tasks he cannot finish, such as counting pots of honey. The size of his brain is frequently called into question – usually by himself – although it is unlikely there is any physical anomaly.

He appears to need to think very carefully before doing anything, but often becomes distracted before he has been able to see a clear path ahead. He sometimes writes notes to help with this; it would seem, however, that they make little sense.

Pooh's forgetfulness and inability to plan ahead generally cause trouble. He built a trap to catch a Heffalump, but then failed either to remember where it was or to signpost it adequately, and so ended up trapped in it himself.

Pooh is well liked and generous, but often this results in problems. On one occasion he decided his friend Eeyore needed a house, but failed to consult Eeyore first and ended up dismantling the house Eeyore had painstakingly built for himself.

Pooh cannot tell left from right, which causes him some confusion. In addition, his cognition appears faulty. Often he knows he needs to think about something, but spends so much time thinking about thinking about it that he fails actually to think about the matter in question. This inattention is noticed within his community; Eeyore, for example, attributes it to a lack of education.

Winnie-the-Pooh is overweight and overly interested in eating, indicating he may also have issues with food, perhaps even an addiction to honey. The clock in his house appears to be stuck at five to eleven, which conveniently is the time he likes to have a snack. However, this may simply be because he hasn't noticed that it is not working or has tried but failed to fix it.

Pooh enjoys making up songs. Interestingly, although he often gets distracted, this is one task he usually manages to complete almost to the end. The noise does cause some distress to his friends and neighbours, however. If he could learn to apply the same degree of attention to a more useful pastime, it would probably be of great help to him in the longer term as well as contributing to the community as a whole.

AD/HD – Predominantly Inattentive Type – the facts

Even though Winnie-the-Pooh and Tigger (see Tigger's case study p. 38) seem exceptionally different in their characters and behaviour, they both meet the diagnostic criteria for the overall category of AD/HD. Each animal, however, meets the criteria for a different subtype. It is the Predominantly Inattentive Type of AD/HD that may be applied to Pooh, this being characterised by a pattern of inatten-  tion rather than hyperactivity–impulsivity (as in Tigger's case). Like Pooh, many sufferers of this type of AD/HD seem to be very dreamy, as if their attention is focused elsewhere. This leads to mistakes at school or work, and means projects are often left unfinished. This subtype is diagnosed when there are symptoms of inattentiveness but the sufferer doesn't behave in a way that could be described as either hyperactive or impulsive.

Prognosis

While AD/HD is believed to be incurable, it is possible with the correct care and treatment for there to be a marked improvement. Many adult sufferers of AD/HD go on to have successful careers. In Pooh's case, the catering industry might provide a suitable working environment in which he could put his passion for food to more constructive use.

Treatment

Pooh would probably benefit from a combination of drug and behaviour therapy. As well as helping him to concentrate, behaviour therapy, which focuses on helping the individual to follow tasks through to the end and set up systems to deal with simple day-to-day tasks, such as remembering where one has put things, would raise Pooh's self-esteem as he would begin to learn how to manage his life more successfully. Adjusting his diet would improve Pooh's mental functioning and would have the added benefit of aiding weight loss. He would then be rather less likely to inconvenience Rabbit – or indeed any underground resident of Hundred Acre Wood – by blocking his front door.

HOW TO SPOT A COMPULSIVE DAY-DREAMER

Do you know a Winnie-the-Pooh? Does this person ...

become easily distracted? ☐

dislike or fail to engage in tasks that require sustained mental effort? ☐

not pay attention, therefore making avoidable mistakes? ☐

appear overly forgetful? ☐

find it difficult to remain focused for even short periods of time? ☐

appear inattentive when being spoken to? ☐

fail to follow instructions, therefore not completing tasks such as homework for school or a project for work? ☐

have difficulty organising themselves? ☐

often misplace things? ☐

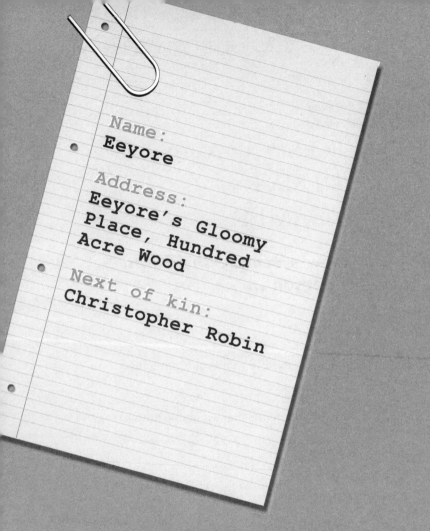

Name:
Eeyore

Address:
**Eeyore's Gloomy
Place, Hundred
Acre Wood**

Next of kin:
Christopher Robin

Therapy might be
all it would take
to lift Eeyore
out of his gloomy
state.

Diagnosis

Dysthymic Disorder (dysphoria)

Eeyore's mood appears depressed and his demeanour downtrodden. The choice of name for his address provides a fitting metaphor for his feelings about life.

Physical presentation

The subject's posture is slumped, his pallor grey and he fidgets with his tail constantly. His eyes are often downcast and his voice low, monotonous and difficult to hear.

Diet

Evidence suggests Eeyore eats only thistles. Therefore his diet lacks the protein, carbohydrates, vitamins, minerals and essential fatty acids necessary for optimum mental and physical health. A change of diet could contribute to recovery.

Family background

Eeyore arrived at Hundred Acre Wood at an early age. No information is available regarding his family history prior to this.

Patient notes

Eeyore lives on the edge of a small community in a state of isolation both geographically and emotionally. It appears he has found it hard to form significant close relationships or to carve out a meaningful and fulfilling role in life.

It would seem that even when in the company of others, Eeyore has a sense of being apart, yet is grateful for any attention. Because he expects so little from life and his fellow creatures, he can be disproportionately pleased by small gestures of kindness – even half-baked ones, such as the empty jar (which should have been full of honey) presented by Pooh on his birthday that delighted him so much because he could keep the (burst) balloon given to him by Piglet in it.

While most of the residents of Hundred Acre Wood have an established pattern of daily life and strong interpersonal relationships, Eeyore occupies the sidelines and has no routine to his life. He would seem to miss out on social opportunities because he hasn't the confidence or motivation to become involved.

Early in his life, Eeyore lost his tail. There is no information on the circumstances of this loss, despite dark rumours that Owl once used it as a bell-rope. It is known that he finds its precarious re-attachment with a nail, rather than by proper surgical procedure, a source of concern. Overall, he views the appendage in question with a mixture of embarrassment and affection. This physical disability may well be at the root of his dysphoria, particularly if it happened during adolescence, when he would have wanted to fit in with his peers and any difference would have been magnified.

Eeyore presents as cynical and sarcastic, hiding underlying low self-esteem and a sense of hopelessness. Evidence suggests he is unable to communicate his needs in a healthy way.

An inability to deal with problems appropriately is likely, such as when he found his house missing. Rather than alerting the community to this disaster, he sought out his friend Christopher Robin and explained the situation in a round-about way, refusing to ask for help or conveying the gravity of the problem. When Christopher Robin asked him what was wrong, Eeyore was circumspect, suggesting it was of no concern. Once the situation was explained to Christopher Robin, however, he was suitably horrified. Again, though, Eeyore minimised the problem. This lack of confidence and self-worth appears all pervasive.

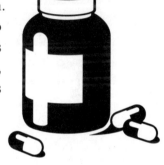

Dysthymic Disorder – the facts

Dysthymic Disorder is characterised by chronic depression lasting for a period of more than two years. Most days, sufferers experience a low mood that tends to persist. It is, however, much less severe than a major depression. To be diagnosed with this disorder there must be no associated mania, hypomania (a milder form of mania) or mixed episodes.

Dysthymic Disorder often starts insidiously, in childhood, adolescence or early adulthood. It's more likely to occur in first-degree relatives (a parent, sibling or child) of those with Major Depressive Disorder.

This disorder has an extremely negative effect on an individual's quality of life. Sufferers often experience a deep feeling of guilt, about many aspects of their life, not just the disorder. Sufferers are also often reluctant to seek help.

Prognosis

Although it is much more usual for a patient with this disorder to be treated at home, in this situation a short inpatient stay would be advisable due to Eeyore's unsatisfactory housing situation. It would, in any case, be inappropriate for Christopher Robin to care for Eeyore during his initial treatment. Although he is now six, he is still young, and to be burdened with such responsibility could cause him emotional problems in later life. As Eeyore is unsatisfactorily housed – constantly losing his home and having to rebuild it – treating him at home would pose additional problems too.

Treatment

A combination of antidepressants and psychotherapy would benefit Eeyore. Fluoxetine (Prozac) has proved very successful in treating Dysthymic Disorder. Eeyore would also benefit from one-to-one psychotherapy, through which issues, including any connected with his childhood, might be explored.

As in the case of Tigger (see p. 38), it is possible that family therapy might be beneficial as this treats the family 'system' rather than just the presenting member. Regular sessions for all the residents of Hundred Acre Wood would allow a therapist to work with the group as a whole and allow them to explore their interconnecting roles.

SPOTTING SOMEONE WITH DYSPHORIA

Is there an Eeyore in your life? Does the person you're concerned about ...

have a poor appetite or overeat? ☐

have trouble sleeping or spend too much time asleep? ☐

seem constantly fatigued? ☐

suffer from low self-esteem? ☐

seem depressed most of the time? ☐

report suffering from this low mood for at least two years? ☐

find it difficult to make decisions? ☐

suffer from feelings of hopelessness? ☐

find it difficult to concentrate? ☐

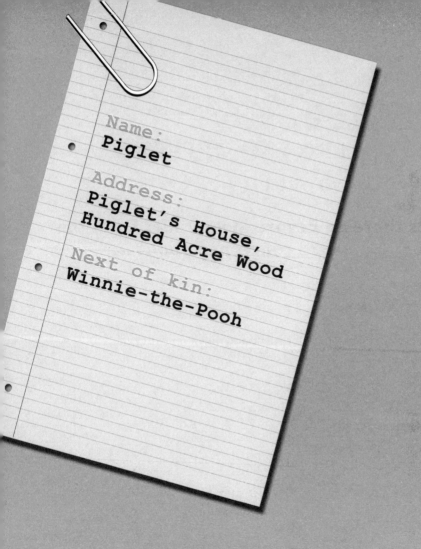

Name:
Piglet

Address:
**Piglet's House,
Hundred Acre Wood**

Next of kin:
Winnie-the-Pooh

Poor Piglet misses out because of his anxious nature.

Piglet

Diagnosis
Generalised Anxiety Disorder (GAD)
Piglet's capacity to enjoy life in Hundred Acre Wood seems hampered by his perpetual timidity and innate nervousness.

Physical presentation
Piglet is nervous, fidgety and appears ill at ease, an impression exacerbated by his squeaky voice and tiny frame. He's hesitant when speaking to his friends and presents as one permanently worried about a potential mishap, *faux pas* or – in his own head at least – disastrous incident.

Diet
Piglet's diet seems to be limited to haycorns. A more varied intake with more fat, protein, vitamins and minerals should be recommended.

Family background
No information is available on Piglet's life before his arrival in Hundred Acre Wood, although a grandfather called Trespassers Will has been mentioned. Unless 'Will' for 'William' indicates a family preference for the diminutive form, the name 'Piglet' suggests that the subject hasn't yet

reached adulthood, so early separation from his parents could well be an issue underlying his condition.

Patient notes

Piglet's inherent timidity and nervousness are always evident. He imagines doom-laden scenarios of mythical beasts and terrible accidents, although he never leaves the familiar, relatively safe territory of the Wood.

For example, when out walking with Pooh on one occasion, he imagined a number of potential disasters that might befall them. Although he wanted to end the walk, he failed to convey his anxiety or his needs to Pooh and continued despite the physical and emotional discomfort he was suffering.

When he and Pooh decided to build Eeyore a house of sticks and – inadvertently – used the sticks that constitute Eeyore's existing house, Piglet was distraught with guilt when the awful mistake became apparent.

There is evidence that his greater worry was that of being 'found out' and it was only when no punishment actually befell them that he seemed able to relax a little and could sing a few more verses of Pooh's favourite snow song.

Piglet's anxiety is so acute that he defers to Pooh, who by his own admission is not the brightest of bears. This actually results in Piglet being exposed to more danger than if he were to rely on his own instincts. Hence, although Piglet has no trouble with cognition, his  uncertainty in himself is self-defeating and causes him to question his intelligence and intuition.

Piglet is overly apologetic. For example, when the pair fell into a trap that Pooh had built to catch Heffalumps, he felt no irritation towards Pooh. In fact, he apologised for being underneath at the moment of impact.

Evidence suggests Piglet's anxiety levels are increased by the presence of disorder. He likes tidiness in his own house, to the extent that he feels it necessary to apologise for his little ways. If plans go awry, his ears twitch, his voice becomes tremulous, he is prone to stuttering, and he becomes physically on edge.

Other residents of Hundred Acre Wood are sensitive to Piglet's issues. Pooh has suggested to Tigger that Piglet might not take kindly to excessive bouncing, while Eeyore – when he can summon the patience – takes the trouble to say things even more slowly when conversing with the nervous Piglet.

Generalised Anxiety Disorder – the facts

Generalised Anxiety Disorder is characterised by excessive anxiety and worry occurring more days than not, over a period of at least six months. Sufferers find it impossible to ameliorate or control their sense of worry, and this increased anxiety is normally accompanied by other symptoms, including restlessness, lack of energy, difficulty concentrating, irritability, muscle tension and disturbed sleep patterns.

Importantly, the sufferer's symptoms are not confined to specific situations or circumstances, such as one that might bring on a panic attack, the anxiety induced by a particular fear or phobia, such as agoraphobia or the fear of being 'contaminated' in some way, as in the case of Obsessive–Compulsive Disorder. More specifically, sufferers will report distress due to constant worry, which is often acknowledged as being disproportionate to the likelihood or potential impact of the feared event.

Adults often worry excessively about routine life circumstances, including job responsibilities, finances, the health of family members, or minor matters such as being late for an appointment or the need to take the car in for a repair.

Children with this disorder typically worry about their own competence or performance.

Prognosis

While Generalised Anxiety Disorder is often a lifelong condition, it does fluctuate in severity. Perhaps not surprisingly, it's often worse during times of stress. With the correct treatment and the understanding of his friends, there is no reason why Piglet's condition could not improve significantly.

Treatment

Most treatment for GAD takes place on an outpatient basis, which would be the most appropriate course for Piglet, although some sufferers may benefit from an inpatient stay. The two main treatments are medication and psychotherapy, either alone or in tandem.

Sedatives or antidepressants may be prescribed – the former to help the sufferer cope with specific episodes by relieving, within a very short timescale, the sense of anxiety, and the latter to provide longer-term support. Among the favoured forms of psychotherapy from which

Piglet may benefit is cognitive behaviour therapy, which examines the distortions in thinking that lead to psychological problems and which can be highly effective in treating anxiety disorders such as GAD.

HOW TO IDENTIFY A CASE OF GENERALISED ANXIETY DISORDER

Do you know someone who is always anxious, just like Piglet?

Have they felt this omnipresent sense of foreboding more days than not for at least six months? ☐

Do they find it difficult to control or manage their anxiety? ☐

Do they worry excessively about seemingly routine matters? ☐

Is their sense of anxiety linked to at least three of the following: restlessness or feeling keyed up; being easily fatigued; difficulty concentrating; irritability; muscle tension; sleep disturbance? ☐

Does it lead to significant distress and/or impairment of day-to-day functioning at work or at home? ☐

Is their anxiety not linked to another psychiatric disorder, such as anorexia nervosa or hypochondriasis? ☐

Is it not a direct result of medication or substance abuse, such as drug or alcohol addiction? ☐

Hundred Acre Wood on the couch

Hundred Acre Wood is a beautiful place. Aside from the occasional natural hazard (trees blowing down, floods, swarms of bees), it offers a safe environment in which to live and, while many of the residents suffer from mental health problems, there is nonetheless a warm community spirit, with residents doing their best to help each other.

There is evidence of occasional housing problems, however. Eeyore has been homeless on more than one occasion and each of the residents – with the exception of Kanga and Roo – lives alone.

The community is more than 90 per cent male, which is highly unusual and could lead to loneliness – quite apart from the issue of who will support an ageing community if there are no offspring to perform this role. Kanga, the only female resident, is bringing up her son, Roo, as a single parent. His father is never mentioned, which may cause problems for him in later life. Nothing is known of why he is absent.

Roo shows signs of hyperactivity and impulsivity. He spends much time with Tigger, so could simply be copying his behaviour. Alternatively, he too could be suffering from AD/HD. Kanga is perhaps overprotective of her son and it is probable that dosing him with extract of malt for medicinal reasons is quite unnecessary.

Owl is intelligent, although probably dyslexic, as evidenced by his frequent misspellings. He also confuses the meaning of words. For example, he believes a 'contradiction' is the opposite of an 'introduction'. His self-esteem is unlikely to be damaged by his literacy problems as none of the residents of Hundred Acre Wood has a real grasp of the written word, indicating that adequate schooling is very much an issue. Owl is widely believed to be not only the wisest, but also the most literate member of the community.

Rabbit can be a little grandiose, although, like Owl, not suffering from any particular disorder. It is possible Rabbit sometimes hurts the feelings of others by being offhand or insulting. Some gentle tuition in diplomacy skills could benefit him.

Christopher Robin is a small boy carrying a heavy weight of responsibility. It is he those who live in Hundred Acre Wood consult on any matter of import. No information is available concerning his parents, although it would appear he has a nanny named Alice. As noted above, too much responsibility at a young age can be bad for a child, however, and could lead to co-dependency (see Wendy, p. 78) later in life. The situation would be better for all if a carer with more experience, hence probably more advanced in years, could take greater responsibility for the welfare of those who live in the Wood.

The Pathologies in Neverland

Although Neverland seems to be located somewhere near Kensington Gardens, it's a world away from the relative sanity of London. This is a dangerous place, with insecure relationships and rampant lawlessness. The residents are continually embroiled in struggles for power, often resulting in loss of life or, in the case of Captain Hook, loss of limb. There rarely seems to be a winner, except perhaps a passing crocodile.

The vast majority of its inhabitants remain childlike, whatever their age, and appear to suffer as a result of a probable failure in infancy to become properly attached to their parents. Although there are many fairies in Neverland, they're not the traditional sort who grant wishes; in fact, they're more likely to dish out punches.

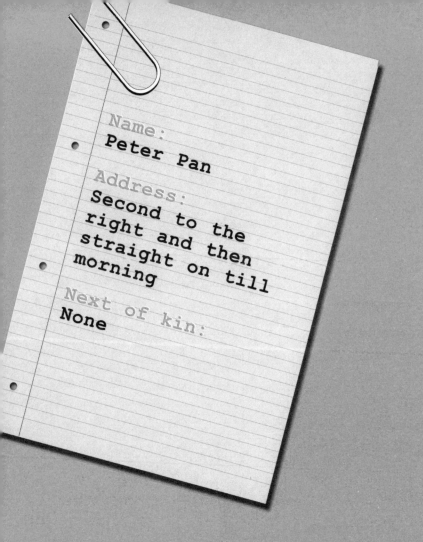

Name:
Peter Pan

Address:
Second to the right and then straight on till morning

Next of kin:
None

'I can't help crowing, Wendy, when I'm pleased with myself.'

Peter Pan

Diagnosis

Unhealthy narcissism and self-defeating, dependent character traits

Peter's grandiose ways and lack of care and empathy make him a danger to himself and to others.

Physical presentation

Peter appears healthy, although he is small. It is difficult to judge his age from his appearance.

Diet

Peter has issues with food. There is evidence of an eating disorder – Peter can eat if it is part of a game, but not just to 'feel full'. Whether there would be a real meal for everyone or only a make-believe one, where all *pretended* to eat, is entirely subject to Peter's whim. Many experts believe eating disorders can stem from a desire to stay a child.

Family background

Peter was born in London. Little is known of his parents due to the fact that he ran away from home the day after his birth having overheard his parents discussing his future and what he might be when he became a man. This distressed Peter greatly since he wanted to stay a child forever, so he left to live with the fairies in Kensington Gardens before any relationship with his parents could become established.

Patient notes

Peter is unwilling to grow up and take on age-appropriate responsibilities. He wants to remain a young boy forever and retains a childlike egocentricity. He refused to tell Wendy his age when asked, suggesting that he feels uncomfortable confronting the whole issue of ageing.

He also finds it difficult to admit that he might have any weakness. When Wendy met him for the first time, sobbing on the nursery floor because he couldn't re-attach his shadow, he denied that he had been crying, soon persuading himself that he had never cried in his life, despite clear evidence to the contrary. Peter uses 'splitting' – dealing with emotional conflict by seeing things either as all good or all bad and not recognising the grey areas in between – as a defence mechanism. On meeting Wendy, for example, he declared that mothers are 'very over-rated persons' and that he had 'not the slightest desire to have one', although his vulnerability was all too apparent.

While denying his need for a mother, he appears on a deeper level to realise he and the Lost Boys – a group of male children who have fallen from their prams and ended up in Neverland – need some kind of nurturing relationship, one that traditionally a mother would provide. He looks to Wendy to meet this need and manipulated her into playing this role by suggesting that girls 'are much too clever to fall out of their prams' and that 'one girl is more use than twenty boys'. It is interesting to note that in making such comments he was appealing to her vanity – a trait that is strong

in him – to persuade her to go to Neverland, a place where there are no responsible adults and the children run wild.

Peter forbids the Lost Boys from looking anything like him. While he wears leaves that are light and easy to move in, they are condemned to dress in bear skins, which he makes them hunt for themselves and which are far less comfortable than the clothes he wears.

Peter requires a lot of attention and is easily bored, causing those around him to become exhausted by his demands. Evidence suggests that when Peter is not present everyday life functions much more normally. In Neverland, the fairies spend more time on themselves, the beasts look after their young more effectively and the violent conflict between the pirates and the Lost Boys is all but forgotten. For Wendy and her brothers, too, things were far safer and more settled before Peter's arrival.

Peter dislikes routine and can be quite contrary; something he would find amusing one day becomes tedious the next. This is common in individuals with destructive narcissistic traits. It leaves those around him feeling confused, as what will please him one day may enrage him the next.

Peter did once attempt to return to his family home, but found the nursery window locked and barred and a boy in his place – presumably his parents went on to have another child after he disappeared. While he doesn't admit it, it's likely he found this very hurtful and it is, perhaps, one of the reasons he holds mothers in such low regard.

Often, when there are strong narcissistic traits in a person, there has been a disturbance in their early care. This is more usually to do with adoption, divorce or illness. As Peter didn't receive consistent care in his first years, it is unsurprising that he has developed such traits.

Narcissism – the facts

Those with narcissistic traits are often very vulnerable. While they may appear rather arrogant, they could be experiencing low self-esteem and can be very sensitive to real or imagined criticism. And while they may be physically and intellectually mature, their emotions have remained child-like. Narcissistic characters are often easily bored and are constantly looking for new adventure or wanting change. This can make them exciting to be around, but also very tiring, as eventually most people want to settle down. Narcissists thrive on attention and will seek it out anywhere they can. If positive attention is unavailable, they will often behave badly, as negative attention is more desirable to them than no attention at all.

Prognosis

While Peter meets the diagnostic criteria for full Narcissistic Personality Disorder, a diagnosis could not be made for NPD as it is impossible to determine his age. Adolescents often have narcissistic traits – as Peter does – and then grow out of them. Sufferers of NPD, however, need to reach adulthood before they can be diagnosed with this disorder. Both those with full NPD and those with narcissistic traits find the implications of ageing very difficult to deal with.

Narcissistic people are often extremely attractive to others, however. Their apparent self-belief can be very seductive and those who live with them tend to remain committed despite the negative aspects of the relationship.

This is because the narcissistic person can at times be very loving and attentive.

Treatment

Psychotherapy would be the most appropriate form of treatment in this case. Peter could learn – with the help of a sympathetic therapist – to overcome his sense of entitlement and to behave in an empathic manner towards others, particularly Tinker Bell, who is emotionally unstable and very obviously in love with him.

Peter's need for praise and his tendency to 'crow' when he feels he's done something well are typically narcissistic. He also shamelessly exploits those around him. For example, spiriting Wendy away from home in order to look after him and the Lost Boys took no account of what would be best for her. Therapy could help him to find more healthy ways to get his needs met, without hurting others.

Narcissism is one of the most difficult character traits to treat, as the patient often believes there is nothing wrong with them, or that the therapist isn't sufficiently competent to treat their 'special' case. Therapists frequently suffer 'burnout' while endeavouring to treat a narcissistic patient, making the process harder still.

HOW TO SPOT A NARCISSIST

Do you know a Peter Pan? Do they ...

behave in an irresponsible fashion? ☐

find grown-up, day-to-day matters boring and difficult to deal with? ☐

find it difficult to pay attention to others? ☐

have problems empathising? ☐

feel envious or begrudge others their achievements? ☐

talk up their achievements or take full credit for a team effort? ☐

exploit others for their own means? ☐

require excessive admiration? ☐

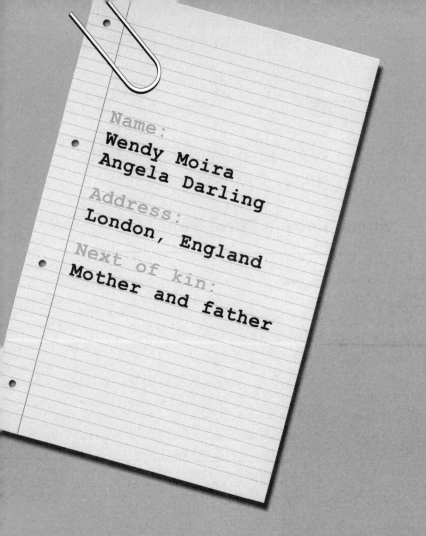

Name:
Wendy Moira Angela Darling

Address:
London, England

Next of kin:
Mother and father

'Once you fit, great care must be taken to go on fitting.'

Wendy

Diagnosis
Co-dependency

Wendy feels the need to take care of those around her, regardless of the effect it has on her own welfare.

Physical presentation
Wendy appears healthy and neat and tidy, suggesting she takes good care of herself.

Diet
Evidence suggests Wendy has a healthy relationship with food, although she is more concerned that others are well nourished.

Family background
Wendy lives with her parents, Mr and Mrs Darling, and her brothers, John and Michael. Mr Darling has strong narcissistic traits (see Peter Pan, p. 70). Mrs Darling appears to mother her children in an appropriate manner.

Patient notes
Wendy has always taken on too much responsibility for her age and, when only two years old, became aware that she must grow up. This was a defining moment for her: 'the beginning of the end'.

Wendy's tendency to 'people please' stops her from living her life authentically. She has both private and public opinions: while her private opinions are sometimes at variance with those of Peter or her father, the public ones never are.

On occasion, if Peter or Mr Darling treat her badly or abuse her good nature, her defence mechanism is to deny this is happening. For example, when her father praised her on one occasion for finding his detested medicine, his sarcasm appeared to pass her by completely.

It is perhaps not surprising that Wendy finds it humiliating to confess that Peter's conceitedness is one of his most fascinating qualities to her. Of course, Mr Darling has similar narcissistic character traits and is often cruel in the way he speaks to his wife and children.

Nothing is too much trouble for Wendy. When she once sewed Peter's shadow back on as a favour, she fretted that perhaps she should have ironed it too.

Wendy's first thought is never for herself. When Peter asked her to fly to Neverland and she initially refused, it was because she felt it might upset her mother. She didn't even consider whether she herself would like it or not, merely how her mother would feel, which is clear evidence of her need to always please others before herself.

Further, if Wendy's father had put his children's needs before his own – and in so doing had built up their self-confidence to an appropriate level – then Wendy may have been more self-respecting and perhaps might have considered more carefully Peter's insistence that she accompany him to Neverland. A child with a positive paternal role model might have found Peter's behaviour alarming and might well have refused to have anything to do with him. Children who live in a disordered environment often have a higher tolerance for inappropriate behaviour in others.

Wendy fears that if she complains about Peter, he will abandon her and her brothers, John and Michael. The brothers dislike Peter's selfishness and egocentricity, complaining that he is always showing off, yet Wendy's response is to tell them: 'You must be nice to him … What could we do if he were to leave us?'

As additional evidence of Wendy's predisposition to see only the good in people, she takes no notice of Tinker Bell's negativity towards her. For example, whenever the fairy's face is distorted with passion and jealousy, Wendy fails to see this and instead exclaims how lovely Tinker Bell looks.

Wendy's concern for her parents, her brothers, for Peter and the Lost Boys, is so strong that she neglects her own feelings entirely. This leaves her open to relationships in which she is in danger of having her needs left unmet and, in more extreme cases, at risk of abuse.

Co-dependency – the facts

While not listed as a disorder in the *Diagnostic and Statistical Manual of Mental Disorders*, co-dependency is a condition many mental health professionals deal with on a daily basis. The condition is most prevalent in the children of addicts, or those with personality disorders or other emotional problems. Many of those affected by it go on to marry or enter into similar co-dependent relationships with individuals suffering from an addiction or other disorder. For children, co-dependency presents as a pattern of behaviour that is overly responsible for their age. They feel they have to 'parent' their own mother, father or siblings and behave in a more grown-up fashion than the adults around them. Co-dependents put the needs of others before their own and often end up feeling depressed and resentful as a result.

Prognosis

Wendy needs to learn to set boundaries and to assert herself so that her needs are properly met. Her desire to please others may well be a way of her trying to get them to meet her needs in return. If Wendy were to commit to treatment there is a good chance she would learn to ask for what she needs.

Treatment

Family therapy may be appropriate in the case of the Darlings. Their relationships with one another could be explored and they could learn to relate to each other and communicate in healthier ways. Wendy may also benefit from a short course of cognitive behaviour therapy, through which she might learn to assert herself and understand that saying 'no' to those you care about will not have disastrous consequences.

HOW TO IDENTIFY A CO-DEPENDENT PERSON

Do you know a Wendy? Does this person ...

find it seemingly impossible to express their needs healthily? ☐

find it difficult to say no? ☐

only feel good about themself when they're doing something for someone else? ☐

allow others to take credit for their endeavours? ☐

feel uncomfortable if they're not needed? ☐

behave too responsibly for their age? ☐

seem more grown-up than the adults they live with? ☐

seem out of touch with their feelings? ☐

need constant reassurance that they're doing a good job? ☐

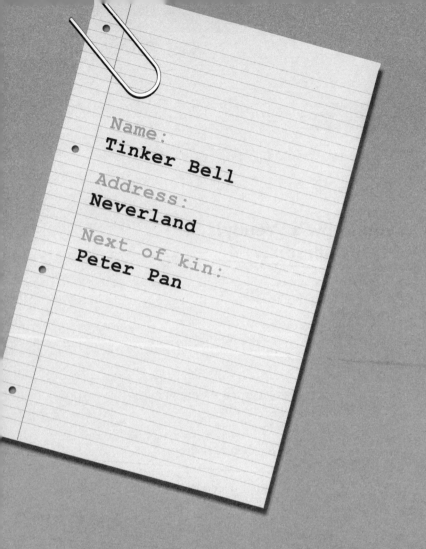

Name:
Tinker Bell
Address:
Neverland
Next of kin:
Peter Pan

'You silly ass!'

Tinker Bell

Diagnosis
Borderline Personality Disorder (BPD)
Tinker Bell is unable to form stable personal relationships and fears Peter will abandon her for Wendy.

Physical presentation
Tinker Bell is embarrassed by her size and this is apparent in her demeanour.

Diet
There is no evidence that Tinker Bell has an unhealthy attitude towards food, although it is not unusual for those with BPD to binge eat or suffer from bulimia.

Family background
Nothing is known of Tinker Bell's family of origin.

Patient notes
Tinker Bell lives in Neverland with Peter Pan and the Lost Boys. She would like to be Peter's fairy, but this is not allowed as she is female and male humans cannot have a fairy of the opposite sex.

Tinker Bell is in love with Peter and becomes extremely jealous when he interacts with Wendy. She finds it difficult to control her emotions and is often verbally abusive and physically violent towards Wendy. On one occasion she took this to extremes when she tried to get one of the Lost Boys to murder Wendy by shooting her with an arrow. When Peter heard of this he banished Tinker Bell, but Wendy, forever thinking of the welfare of others, made sure this was only a temporary measure.

Sometimes Tinker Bell is all good and sometimes she is all bad. Fairies have to be one thing or the other, at any one time. This is because they are so small and therefore have room for only one feeling at a time. It is common for those with BPD to feel this way as they have an unstable sense of self and can interpret normal, time-limited separation from individuals they care about as rejection or a sign that they are in some way 'bad'.

Tinker Bell finds it seemingly impossible to control her anger. She has violent rages in response to things that would cause only minor irritation in others. Wendy's compassion makes Tinker Bell even more jealous and angry – perhaps because she is incapable of consistently feeling such warmth for another person.

Suicide attempts and self-harm are common in those with BPD, as are reckless and impulsive acts. When Peter's medicine was poisoned by Captain Hook, Tinker Bell drank it, knowing it might kill her. It was only Peter's intervention that saved her. While it's impossible to say whether Tinker Bell wanted to die, by drinking the medicine she behaved in an irrational way. It would initially appear her motive was to save Peter; equally, it could be seen as a suicide attempt or at least a cry for attention.

Borderline Personality Disorder – the facts

The prospect of real or imagined rejection lies at the heart of this disorder, along with a disturbed sense of self. Those with BPD have a propensity to undermine themselves just as a goal is about to be achieved, such as dropping out of university immediately before graduation. In Tinker Bell's case, she drank the poisoned medicine just as Wendy was about to leave Neverland, allowing the fairy to have Peter to herself again.

Sometimes a sufferer of BPD may experience a dissociative state. A dissociative state occurs when a person's feelings, perceptions and memories become disconnected from each other, or no longer register in the conscious mind. This causes their sense of who they are, and the way they perceive the world around them, to alter significantly.

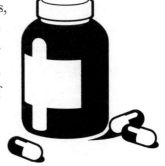

Around 75 per cent of those diagnosed with BPD are female, although this may be because women are more likely to seek help.

Prognosis

If Tinker Bell were to commit to regular, long-term therapy, there is a good chance she might see an improvement in her condition. Moreover, many patients report a reduction in symptoms once they are in their forties. Obviously, Tinker Bell is an extreme case; she has, after all, coerced a Lost Boy into attempting to murder Wendy. Personality disorders exist along a broad spectrum and clearly Tinker Bell is at the extreme edge of this.

Treatment

Long-term psychotherapy would be recommended for Tinker Bell. Should she attempt suicide again or continue to be a danger to others, an inpatient stay in a psychiatric hospital would probably be advisable. Drugs can be used to treat any accompanying depression and medication such as carbamazepine could be used to stabilise her moods and regulate her emotions. This could be particularly useful in calming her jealous rages.

HOW TO SPOT SOMEONE WITH BPD

Do you know a Tinker Bell? Do they do five or more of the following:

struggle in relationships, either idealising their partner or devaluing them? ☐

have an unstable or unrealistic sense of who they are or how they appear to others? ☐

behave in a reckless or self-damaging way with regard to sex, drugs, alcohol or food or shopping? ☐

strive to avoid a feeling of abandonment, whether real or imagined? ☐

demonstrate significant fluctuations in mood, frequently feeling anxious or irritable, or showing signs of dysphoria (see Eeyore, p. 52)? ☐

complain of feeling empty for a sustained period of time? ☐

experience episodes of rage of an intensity that is disproportionate to whatever triggered the anger? ☐

self-harm, or frequently hint at, threaten or attempt suicide? ☐

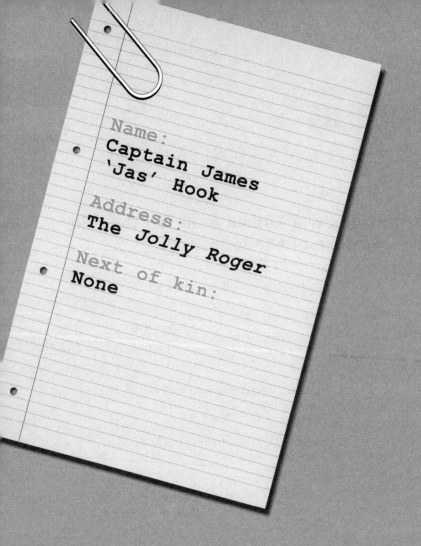

Name:
**Captain James
'Jas' Hook**

Address:
The Jolly Roger

Next of kin:
None

'Cleave him to
the brisket!'

Captain Hook

Diagnosis

Antisocial Personality Disorder

Hook's antisocial behaviour masks a deep-seated unhappiness.

Physical presentation

Captain Hook is well dressed. He has long hair and a cadaverous look about him. Having lost his right hand during a fight with Peter Pan (who fed it to a crocodile), he now wears a prosthetic hook in its place. His demeanour is one of sinister politeness.

Diet

Nothing is known of Hook's relationship with food or his diet, but his appearance doesn't suggest any malnutrition.

Family background

Nothing is known of Hook's background, apart from his having been sent away to boarding school as a child.

Patient notes

As a pirate, Captain Hook lives the life of a criminal. He enjoys being feared, often boasting of the terror he evokes in others.

He has no friends, only his crew, whom he treats and addresses as if they were a pack of dogs. And, like dogs, they blindly follow him with unstinting loyalty, although his attitude to them is dismissive and snobbish.

As a child, Hook attended boarding school. Since punishments of the time were brutal and regimes harsh, this may have contributed to the onset of his disorder. It is thought this particular personality disorder can be brought on by unstable or erratic parenting and inconsistent disciplining. It is likely there would have been a marked difference in his home and school lives.

Although he takes pride in his iron claw, Captain Hook passionately wants revenge on Peter Pan for depriving him of his hand. He is willing to do anything to kill Peter and uses his crew and anyone else he comes into contact with to help him achieve this aim.

His violence is usually directed at those weaker than himself. For instance, he took sadistic pleasure in his plans to make Wendy watch the Lost Boys and her brothers walk the plank. He also tormented the children, with insincere promises of making two of them cabin boys, before attempting to send them to their deaths.

Hook is unscrupulous and conducts his attacks improperly. He goes against the rules of warfare, despite being fully aware of them. In a fight with Peter, Hook bit him on the hand – an act of gross unfairness in Peter's eyes when he had been trying to help the pirate in order to ensure fair play. Later, Hook also tried to poison the boy as he slept.

Interestingly, on one occasion when his men momentarily lost faith in him, Hook felt his usually unassailable self-confidence begin to ebb, he spoke directly to his flagging ego, saying: 'Don't desert me, bully.'

Hook also suffers from bouts of dysphoria (see Eeyore, p. 52), which is common in those with Antisocial Personality Disorder. When he walks the deck of his ship at night, he often feels profoundly alone and dejected.

Antisocial Personality Disorder – the facts

Those with Antisocial Personality Disorder often lack empathy and frequently ignore, or are disdainful of, the feelings of others. They can believe themselves to be superior, as if laws or rules do not apply to them. Sufferers rarely have a clear plan of where their life is going. They tend to quit jobs before thinking through what they might do next and are often unemployed, even when suitable jobs are available.

Aggression is frequently part of the disorder. Sufferers may pick fights with strangers or attack those they know. Often they are also financially irresponsible, falling into debt or failing to support their dependants.

Prognosis

Success in the treatment of Antisocial Personality Disorder is limited. Symptoms, however, may become less pronounced as the individual grows older. Captain Hook is unlikely ever to seek treatment for this; however, as those who suffer from this disorder have a low tolerance for emotional pain, he might seek help to deal with his depressive symptoms if they were to become unbearable. Even so, it is extremely unlikely he would stay the course and explore the issues underlying his depression.

Treatment

Those with Antisocial Personality Disorder rarely seek help themselves. It is more usual for them to come into the mental health system as a consequence of a court order. Psychotherapy is usually the treatment of choice, but achieving a successful therapist/patient relationship can be difficult. It is, of course, unlikely that Hook would ever end up in the legal system, as Neverland doesn't have one.

HOW TO IDENTIFY AN ANTISOCIAL PERSONALITY

Do you know a Captain Hook? Can you answer 'yes' to more than three of the following questions? Do they ...

become easily irritated or angry, to the point of physical aggression? ☐

frequently break the law? ☐

show little regard for their own wellbeing or that of others? ☐

repeatedly lie or deceive for personal gain or amusement? ☐

show a complete disregard for or indifference towards those they have treated badly? ☐

behave in reckless and thoughtless fashion, with no regard to the consequences of their actions? ☐

appear reluctant to plan for the future? ☐

show an irresponsible disregard for the need to behave appropriately in the workplace or to honour financial commitments? ☐

Neverland on the couch

Neverland is an unhealthy place to live. It lacks structure and the residents have developed inappropriate coping mechanisms. There is no democracy but, equally, no one is in charge. The power struggle between Peter Pan and Captain Hook affects the whole community and residents find themselves doing the unthinkable in order to try and keep some semblance of peace or order. Captain Hook's crew, for example, are willing to make children walk the plank, simply to please him.

Without an education system in place, the Lost Boys and, latterly, the Darling children, learn from example, whether good or bad. The examples set by the few adults in Neverland are inappropriate and often dangerous. And since there are no good role models, many of the Lost Boys and at least one of the Darling children have a hankering to become a pirate and lead a lawless life. This could be an indication of Stockholm Syndrome – an emotional attachment formed by a hostage for a captor as a result of a need for survival – but is more likely just the game-playing of young boys.

Wendy's desire to mother the children of Neverland could perhaps be seen as a need to control her external environment because of the sense of disorder she feels at home. Supervision of the Darling children's physical and emotional wellbeing is largely left in the paws of the (albeit highly competent) family dog, Nana, which must contribute in part to Wendy's need for a more conventional domestic set-up.

The Lost Boys' lack of consistent care at an early age may well cause problems in later life. Much of a child's emotional development takes place during the first two years and it is important that the child should be made to feel secure and loved during this period. As the Lost Boys came to Neverland having fallen from their prams, it is likely they would have arrived during their first year and there would have been no opportunity for them to form secure attachments to adults. There is also every possibility they could develop anxiety disorders as a result of the violence they have witnessed.

Once in Neverland, Wendy's brothers, John and Michael, seemed to forget their parents and their lives at home, a state of affairs that Wendy finds most disturbing. John sometimes vaguely remembers his parents as people he once knew, while Michael believes Wendy is his mother. This dissociative state may well have been brought on by the stress of leaving home suddenly. Both boys experienced much emotional trauma while in Neverland, including being kidnapped and seeing their sister shot with an arrow. Wendy has tried to cure the boys' amnesia by setting them exams on their parents.

Many of the problems in Neverland are caused by a lack of consistent and healthy parenting of its juvenile residents. An audit by social services might well recommend that the foster-parenting model be adopted in order to help the younger residents become better adjusted. Suitable foster parents are unlikely to be found in Neverland.

The Pathologies in Oz

The Land of Oz is an extraordinary place with a vast population, many of whom are suffering on an emotional and psychological level. The good news is that with the right help and support, a large proportion of them are actually well on their way to recovery.

For the Lion, the Tin Woodman, the Scarecrow and indeed Dorothy, the quest to find the Wizard and be granted the things they most want in life is perhaps a little like undergoing therapy – a journey of self-exploration leading to better understanding of their personal needs and increased self-confidence.

In the end the four friends discover that, while it was necessary to seek help, ultimately the ability to achieve what they wanted was inside them all the time.

Name:
The Wizard of Oz.
(The Wizard's full name –
Oscar Zoroaster Phadrig
Isaac Norman Henkle
Emmanuel Ambroise Diggs –
has always been a source of
embarrassment to him, as
his initials spell OZ
PINHEAD. He has thus short-
ened it to 'Oz')

Address:
**The Emerald City,
the Land of Oz**

Next of kin:

'I am Oz, the
Great and
Terrible.'

The Wizard of Oz

Diagnosis
Narcissistic Personality Disorder (NPD)
The Wizard presents a falsely grandiose image of himself in order to hide his painful feelings of shame and inadequacy.

Physical presentation
The Wizard, on first acquaintance, seems haughty and imperious, constantly changing his outward appearance according to whoever he is speaking to, but always striving to strike a measure of fear into the onlooker. On closer inspection, however, he reveals himself to be a small, elderly, bald-headed gentleman with rather less bite than his initial 'bark' would suggest.

Diet
From his time in Oz, the Wizard has become used to having his every culinary whim catered for. Without minions to provide for him, it is unlikely he would be able to satisfy even the most basic of his nutritional needs.

Family background
The Wizard grew up in Omaha, Nebraska, USA. He has no contact with family members, is unmarried and lives alone.

The Wizard spent his early life in Omaha. On reaching maturity he became a ventriloquist and claims to have been trained by a 'great master'. He boasts of being able to imitate any kind of bird or beast and uses his ability to project his voice in order to present a deceptively intimidating image of himself.

He admits that, ever since arriving in the Land of Oz, he has taken advantage of the good nature of its residents, without a thought for how this might affect them or disrupt the status quo. Upon his arrival – appearing 'magically' out of the clouds in a hot-air balloon – he was greeted as a 'great Wizard' by the people, inhabitants of a nation that was clearly not as technologically advanced as his.

The Wizard says that he saw no reason to disabuse the people of Oz of the idea that he was indeed their new leader, seemingly regarding such adulation as his 'due' and wallowing in the sensation of power: 'Of course I let them think [I was a Wizard], because they were afraid of me, and promised to do anything I wished them to.' He claims he then blatantly exploited the people of Oz, demanding they build a new city for him: 'Just to amuse myself, and keep the good people busy.'

To underline the extent of his control over them, and again demonstrating his failure to treat them as individuals, the Wizard ordered all his subjects to be fitted with green glasses, each pair fastened permanently with a small key. He then named the new metropolis Emerald City, reflecting the fact that its residents perceived everything as green through their compulsory spectacles.

All the Wizard's relationships are superficial. He uses technology to ensure no one sees him as he really is and to keep the people in thrall to him. Using elaborate props, he devises beautiful or terrifying creatures and then, using his ventriloquism skills, throws his voice across the room so it seems to come from the creature in question. He routinely treats the residents of Oz in a dictatorial and exploitative manner, while maintaining that they have everything they need to make them happy.

During his early years in Oz, the Wizard discovered the existence of witches who possess magical powers. Two of the witches used their power in an evil manner and two for good. The Wizard admits to finding the witches intimidating. He claims to have been terrified that their real powers would expose him as a fraud and that the two wicked witches might then have destroyed him.

Having been 'unmasked' by Dorothy and her friends, the Wizard has decided to leave Oz and return to Omaha. He claims to be worried about the reaction of his subjects, should they become aware that he is only a 'common man'. But this is his only concern; he otherwise shows no remorse for his past deception.

Narcissistic Personality Disorder – the facts

This disorder is characterised by a pervasive pattern of grandiosity, need for admiration and lack of empathy, and typically begins in early adulthood. Narcissistic traits are common in teenagers and don't necessarily indicate that a disorder is present (for more on this, see Peter Pan, p. 70).

The vast majority of NPD sufferers are men, although it is estimated that under 1 per cent of the general population suffers from it. Narcissistic Personality Disorder is emotionally painful, both for the sufferer and for those who are close to him.

Individuals with NPD have difficulty recognising the feelings, subjective experiences, concerns and needs of others. This makes maintaining close relationships difficult. Reports suggest a greater likelihood of heritability than with other personality disorders.

Those suffering from this disorder require excessive attention from other people and consequently feel uncomfortable when others seem to be stealing the limelight. They have an unstable sense of self and are preoccupied with fantasies of unlimited success, power and brilliance.

Oz has almost certainly spent his entire life behaving in a narcissistic fashion and hiding from his true feelings. Underneath he's likely to feel vulnerable, unworthy and lost. He's projected a false image of himself for so long, he surely feels confused about his true identity.

Those close to a person with NPD often find the disorder more difficult to cope with than the sufferer does themself. As a result, relationships with narcissists tend to be unstable, leaving the non-narcissistic partner confused and with low self-esteem. The partner or spouse knows something is very wrong, but are not sure quite what. They have a feeling they're not in Kansas any more, but are unsure how to get back.

Prognosis

The likelihood of recovery or even improvement in individuals with NPD is poor. It is unusual for sufferers to seek help. If they do present for treatment, it's usually at the behest of a partner or relative, and then most tend to drop out, often questioning the therapist's worth. The Wizard's age, and the fact that he has been treated as a king for so long, will perhaps further impede any chances of recovery.

Treatment

Psychotherapy is the most effective means of treating Narcissistic Personality Disorder. However, its effects are limited. The patient needs to follow a long-term programme, usually lasting for a number of years. It is extremely unusual for a sufferer to do this, as they tend to have a low boredom threshold and find it difficult to commit to the rigours of long-term therapy.

Cognitive Behaviour Therapy can be very effective in teaching the sufferer how to cope with situations in a more appropriate manner. For example, the Wizard might revisit situations where he had behaved exploitatively and explore the probable outcomes of a different course of action for both himself and others. As with psychotherapy, its success is dependent on the patient lasting the course. The Wizard might seek help for any immediate depression he may feel at having to live a 'normal' life back in Omaha, but once the depression had lifted, it is unlikely he would continue therapy in order to investigate the underlying causes of his disorder.

Medication cannot cure a personality disorder and should never be used in place of therapy. However, many patients find it easier to engage with therapy while taking medication in order to help lift any accompanying depression or modify impulsive behaviour. Three types of drug are used for Narcissistic Personality Disorder: antidepressants, anticonvulsants and antipsychotics. Unsurprisingly, it is often difficult to get the patient to commit to taking medication, even on a fairly short-term basis.

HOW TO IDENTIFY SOMEONE WITH NPD

Do you know a Wizard of Oz? Does the person in question ...

exaggerate their ability and expect those around them to regard them as superior, without ever having done anything to prove this? ☐

believe they are uniquely special and should only mix in with those of superior social standing? ☐

feel a pervading sense of entitlement and therefore have an unreasonable expectation to be treated with particular respect? ☐

fantasise obsessively about physical appearance, intelligence, success, power or the perfect relationship? ☐

take advantage of others to achieve their own ends? ☐

feel a constant need to be admired? ☐

lack empathy – being unwilling to recognise or identify with the needs and feelings of others? ☐

show envy or believe that others are envious of them? ☐

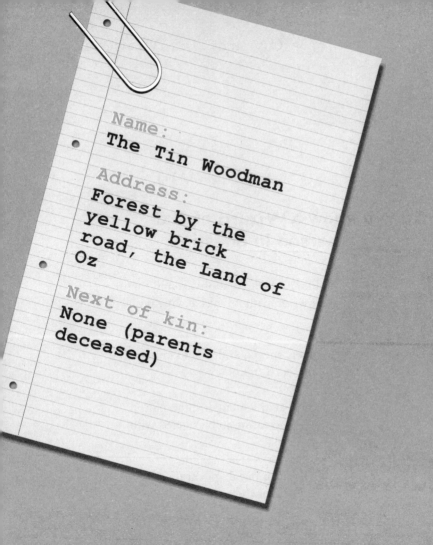

Name:
The Tin Woodman

Address:
Forest by the yellow brick road, the Land of Oz

Next of kin:
None (parents deceased)

'The greatest loss I had known was the loss of my heart.'

The Tin Woodman

Diagnosis
Schizoid Personality Disorder (SPD)
The Tin Woodman's belief that he is unable to love causes him to spend his life alone.

Physical presentation
The Tin Woodman appears stiff and uncomfortable. On occasion his joints seize up entirely.

Diet
He has little interest in food, though it's known he likes to be 'well oiled'.

Family background
The Tin Woodman grew up in an isolated location with his mother and father. He lived at home until each of his parents had passed away.

Patient notes
Despite experiencing early loss – the Tin Woodman's parents died within a few years of each other – he seemed to cope well, although in a fairly detached manner. All indications suggest he had an otherwise happy childhood. He followed his father's career and became a woodsman.

109

Desiring companionship following the death of his parents, he became engaged to a Munchkin girl and the relationship appeared stable.

It was at this point that the Tin Woodman's life became marred by violence. His body, as a result of a series of violent assaults, has been almost entirely rebuilt from tin. The trauma of this may well have exacerbated, or even triggered, his disorder.

The attacks were carried out by the Wicked Witch of the East, who was paid – in the form of livestock – by the employer of the Tin Woodman's fiancée, to put a stop to the forthcoming marriage. Each attack resulted in loss of limb and replacement by a body part of 'unfeeling' metal. With the loss, finally, of his heart – literally and metaphorically – the Tin Woodman found that he no longer loved his fiancée and so called off the engagement. It's clear that the Tin Woodman now finds it impossible to separate the feeling of love from that of pain, and this has caused him to cut himself off from his emotions.

He states he was happy and very proud of his shiny new body at first, although it's possible that this is because he regarded it as a sort of shield from further harm ('it did not matter now if my axe slipped, for it could not cut me'), hiding deep unhappiness within.

When he recounts his troubles, the Tin Woodman does so without emotion. It is telling, however, that, despite his impassive demeanour, he still recognises the importance of emotional fulfilment, rating this higher even than intelligence, as he has made clear to the Scarecrow: '… brains do not make one happy … happiness is the best thing in the world.'

It was when he got caught in the rain and his joints rusted, rendering him completely paralysed for a whole year, that he arrived at this conclusion. He now realised that his life would be better if he had a heart again and could love, thus prompting him to visit the Wizard of Oz to ask for help. One might say that having arrived at this positive decision, the journey towards self-healing, initiated by that year of enforced inactivity and vital self-analysis, had already begun. Not every sufferer of this disorder is as lucky.

Schizoid Personality Disorder – the facts

Schizoid Personality Disorder is characterised by the sufferer's inability or lack of desire to interact with others and their propensity to avoid social situations. Often they appear to lack emotional depth or seem aloof, boring or without humour. However, inside this emotional 'armour' they may feel in turmoil and full of unmet needs. Perhaps – like the Tin Woodman – some sufferers of this disorder really crave emotional intimacy, but seek isolation as a way of not having to deal with the painful aspects of relationships.

Prognosis

Those suffering from SPD are uncomfortable relating to others and rarely seek help. Therefore their condition seldom improves. The Tin Woodman is one of the minority able to see they urgently need help, and he seeks it – albeit in an unconventional way. A psychiatrist – someone with proper medical training – is likely to be much more beneficial to him than the Wizard (whose 'complementary' methods many would dismiss as sheer hocus-pocus), but the mere fact he recognises and accepts he needs help is a good starting point and indicates he may well go on to lead a more fulfilling life.

Treatment

While no drugs are designed specifically to treat SPD, certain medications can help with specific symptoms or social problems, such as nervousness in interpersonal relationships or the inability to form romantic attachments. Psychotherapy can also prove effective, particularly Cognitive Behaviour Therapy, which can help those with this disorder learn how to interact more effectively with others. For example, it can teach the sufferer how to 'read' other people's moods more accurately and perhaps not always assume a negative response will be forthcoming.

HOW TO SPOT SOMEONE WITH A SCHIZOID PERSONALITY

Do you know someone who feels like the Tin Woodman? Do they ...

have no, nor seem to want, close relationships with other people? ☐

prefer solitary pursuits? ☐

seem disinclined to become involved with people for romantic or sexual purposes? ☐

not seem to enjoy many, or indeed any, activities? ☐

have no close friends other than family members? ☐

seem indifferent to other people's opinion, whether negative or positive? ☐

appear cold and detached? ☐

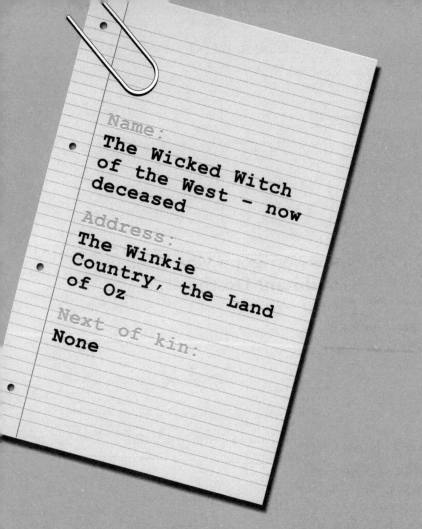

Name:
The Wicked Witch of the West — now deceased

Address:
The Winkie Country, the Land of Oz

Next of kin:
None

'The Wicked Witch was so angry … she stamped her foot and tore her hair and gnashed her teeth.'

Case study

The Wicked Witch
of the West

Diagnosis

Intermittent Explosive Disorder and strong narcissistic traits

The Wicked Witch was unable to control her anger to such an extent that she caused a great degree of harm to others.

Family background

Not much is known of the Witch's family. It is possible that the Wicked Witch of the East was her sister, who – due to a freak accident with a flying shed – is also now dead.

Physical presentation

The Wicked Witch had only one eye, but this had the range of a telescope. Arguably, this was not such an advantage, however, as the images it presented to her view only served to fuel her anger.

Diet

Nothing is known of the Witch's diet, although she was highly allergic to water – fatally so, as it was to prove.

The Witch was easily angered, especially by intrusions into what she regarded as her own territory. She was unable to control her impulses to such a degree that situations other people may have found mildly irritating would drive her over the edge and cause her to lash out violently and with a complete lack of self-control.

The extraordinary extent to which she could be enraged is evidenced by her reaction to the arrival of Dorothy and her companions in the Winkie Country, an area of Oz she regarded as her own. Seeing them as a threat, as she would have done any stranger, she immediately ordered their murder, devising ever more extravagant ways of killing them as each attempt on their lives failed, and becoming ever more furious with each successive failure.

To enforce her violent and impetuous demands, the Witch had at her command an 'army' of fierce creatures. Everyone who lived in the Winkie Country – and all those who visited – inevitably became enslaved by her, as her rages were so ferocious and she was so well defended, they were powerless to fight back. Those who refused to comply with her wishes were brutally murdered.

Though the Witch had a grandiose sense of self-worth,

she did acknowledge there were others in Oz who were equally or more powerful. She did not dare to attack Dorothy, for instance, seeing that she had been protected by a charmed kiss from the good Witch of the North. She felt uncomfortable admitting such weakness even to herself, however, failing to recognise that it might lie behind her obsession for defending herself from perceived attack.

Intermittent Explosive Disorder – the facts

This disorder is characterised by self-contained episodes where the sufferer fails to resist aggressive impulses. This can manifest as road rage, domestic violence or, in the case of the Wicked Witch of the West, a violent reaction to anyone visiting what she considers to be her country. The degree of aggression shown during an episode is, crucially, wholly out of proportion to any provocation.

Prognosis

Obviously, due to her demise, there is no hope of recovery for the Witch. In some individuals, Intermittent Explosive Disorder is a lifelong problem. In others it is more episodic, however, perhaps  brought on by stressful events, and hence there is a better chance of successful treatment.

This disorder is commonly seen in those with a full-blown Narcissistic Personality Disorder (see the Wizard of Oz, p. 100) or strong narcissistic traits (see Peter Pan, p. 70). Indeed it is common, under these circumstances, for explosive episodes to be referred to as 'narcissistic rages'. It is possible the Witch was also suffering from NPD, but not enough is known to be able to accurately make this diagnosis.

Treatment

Treatment for this disorder usually involves a combination of drugs and therapy. A number of different medications can be helpful in preventing explosive episodes, including antidepressants and anticonvulsants to help regulate the patient's moods and emotions, and benzodiazapines (a form of tranquilliser) to ease their anxiety. Cognitive Behaviour Therapy might be considered too, in addition to classes for anger or rage management.

HOW TO SPOT A PERSON WITH AN EXPLOSIVE PERSONALITY

Do you know someone who behaves like the Wicked Witch of the West? Have they ...

experienced a degree of aggression grossly out of proportion to events or stresses that preceded the outburst?

given in to the impulse to be aggressive on several unconnected occasions, resulting in violent assaults on others or damage to property?

been able to rule out any other mental or physical disorder that might better explain the aggressive episodes?

The Land of Oz
on the couch

The Land of Oz is vast and varied; some areas are lush and fertile, while others are dry and barren. Oz has an unusually large number of terrifying creatures, including vicious wolves, giant spiders and monstrous Kalidahs (with the body of a bear and the head of a tiger). There are many dangers in Oz, and most of its regions are governed by disordered individuals with narcissistic and violent tendencies who rule without democracy. Some areas were previously taken by force, including Munchkin Land, by the Wicked Witch of the East, and the Winkie Country, by the Wicked Witch of the West, although since the deaths of the two witches, both of these areas have now been liberated. The third, large conurbation – the Emerald City – was created simply to fulfil the narcissistic needs of its ruler, the Wizard of Oz.

The disorders suffered by the inhabitants of Oz are as varied as its landscape. The Lion is a rather confused creature suffering from an anxiety disorder the roots of which are unknown. However, as he appears to be quite sensitive, it could be that environmental factors have contributed to his condition. He's afraid of everything, yet feels at the same time a sense of shame and humiliation at his lack of expected leonine bravery. He masks his feelings of fear and insecurity with aggression, growling and lunging at any other creature he encounters. The fact that he acknowledges his problems and is willing to discuss them with others is a positive sign that he may gain confidence in the long term, however. He also recognised he needed outside intervention for what he describes as his lack of courage and hence decided to visit the Wizard for help.

Although, through facing up to his fears, his sense of negative self-worth appears to have been greatly diminished, this may need reinforcing. A short course of Cognitive Behaviour Therapy and some assertiveness training would thus be of great benefit to him. He could learn how to state his needs clearly and without aggression, and to come to terms with the fact that all lions need not be the same. He will be valued for who he is and respected, in his newfound self-confidence, as 'King of the Forest'.

The Scarecrow struggles with feelings of inadequacy. Abandoned soon after his creation by the Munchkin farmers, he feels less mentally able than those around him. He believes he has no brain yet he fails to recognise that all of his motor functions work well and that his ability to reason is not impaired. The Scarecrow was designed to be precisely that – a figure of straw for frightening the birds – so perhaps this lack of a sense of real purpose is born out of limited and unfulfilling career expectations. Group therapy would work well for him as he would be able to explore his feelings of failure in a safe and supportive environment.

The two good witches, of the North and South, could perhaps be struggling with co-dependency issues (see also Wendy, p. 78). They seem always to be serving others and never putting their own needs first. It would be better for them and the Land of Oz as a whole if they concentrated on themselves for a while, working out what they really want and need in order for them not to burn out or suffer as a result of repressing any feelings of resentment.

The Munchkin people have a well-developed society which seems free from conflict. If they are able to set up a democratic government now they have been released from the despotism of the Wicked Witch of the East, it would be good for their emotional and spiritual wellbeing, as well as their mental health, as they would have the opportunity to further the causes of things that are important to them as a people.

Those who live in the Emerald City have the difficult job of recovering from life in an abusive dictatorship in which every aspect of their lives has been closely controlled. They have lived in fear of the Wizard for many years and, now that he has gone, will need to learn to cope with the fact that much of what they held to be true is not so in reality. For example, their belief that everything in the Emerald City is green, despite the fact that it is an illusion, may be difficult for them to give up and could cause emotional and psychological problems.

Dorothy Gale, a visitor to Oz, copes well with the vagaries of the land. This is due mainly to her stable upbringing by her aunt and uncle. Although she is disturbed to be alone in a foreign place, she interacts appropriately with each individual she meets. For example, when people treat her well, she is polite and kind, but when she experiences rudeness or unfairness, she stands up for herself and maintains strong personal boundaries (very much in the way that Alice does when visiting Wonderland – see p. 30). She is able to use sound cognitive reasoning to overcome many of the problems she faces.

There are many in each of the regions of the Land of Oz who have witnessed cruelty and violence, and they should be closely monitored for signs of excessive anxiety or Post-traumatic Stress Disorder. However, the fact that the various despots and dictators have now been overthrown, and other threats dealt with, bodes well for the physical safety and future mental health of the population.

In the Waiting Room...

Wouldn't it be great if life were a fairy tale? On further consideration, perhaps not. After all, so many of our favourite fictional characters, far from leading an idyllic, carefree life, are in fact in need of some pretty intensive therapy. The foundations of many disorders lie in early childhood and when you look at the formative years of many of these characters, it's not difficult to see how they've ended up suffering. However, with the right diagnosis and proper support, there's every chance that many of these fairy-tale case studies will find a happy ending'.

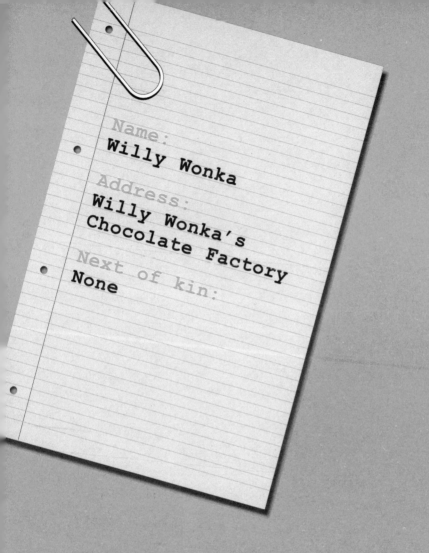

Name:
Willy Wonka

Address:
**Willy Wonka's
Chocolate Factory**

Next of kin:
None

Willy Wonka is
isolated and
increasingly out of
touch with reality.

Willy Wonka

Diagnosis

Schizotypal Personality Disorder

Willy Wonka's paranoia and eccentric behaviour cause difficulties in his personal life.

Physical presentation

Willy Wonka dresses in a flamboyant fashion, wearing a black top hat and plum-coloured tailcoat to work – more like the ringmaster of a circus than what one might expect from the head of a company. Excitable in manner, he makes repeated jerky movements with his head and dances around while talking.

Diet

Evidence suggests Willy Wonka has a healthy diet, which includes fish and vegetables. It is not known if he eats meat. He does, however, have some strange ideas about food; he believes, for example, that breakfast cereal is made of pencil sharpenings and vitamin H can cause one to grow horns.

Family background

Nothing is known of Willy Wonka's family of origin.

Patient notes

Willy Wonka lives and spends most of his time alone. He owns and runs a confectionery factory. He sees no one, apart from his workforce of Oompa-Loompas, people he claims to have smuggled into the country in packing cases. Mr Wonka asserts he discovered them in their native country, a place he calls Loompaland and which no one else has any knowledge of.

Willy Wonka has no familial, personal or social relationships and keeps the doors to his factory chained shut. Previously, he had a more usual workforce, but after secret chocolate recipes were leaked to a competitor, he became paranoid, ordered all staff to leave and halted production at the plant for some time.

He runs the factory along entirely unconventional lines. Rather than worrying primarily about functionality, he insists, for instance, that all the rooms are beautiful, as he cannot abide ugliness. To this end, there are trees and bushes in the factory – all edible – and rivers of chocolate running through it, which are sucked up by pipes and distributed around the factory. He believes the only proper way to mix chocolate is by waterfall.

Willy Wonka responds inappropriately to health and safety issues. Four children have been involved in freak industrial accidents while taking a tour round his factory and on each occasion he found only humour in the situation. He seems entirely unconcerned about any trauma experienced by the children and their families or that he might soon have an expensive lawsuit on his hands as a result of the injuries sustained by the children.

His unconventional way of running a factory is also reflected in his method of recruiting a successor to take over from him when he retires. Rather than advertising for a new member of staff in the usual fashion, he decided to invite five children, winners of a competition, to his factory and hand over the entire company to the child he liked best. According to him, a child is much more likely to learn his way of doing things than an adult, who would try to impose their own ideas – and, by implication, represent far more of a threat to his emotional stability.

His method of conducting the competition – by hiding five special tickets inside chocolate wrappers and leaving the whole matter to chance rather than careful selection based upon merit – is typically cavalier, while perhaps also reflecting a desire to put off the moment of direct contact between himself and his successor.

Schizotypal Personality Disorder – the facts

This disorder is characterised by an acute discomfort about forming close relationships, cognitive and perceptual distortions and a pattern of eccentric behaviour, often leading the sufferer to become isolated. Those with the disorder frequently entertain seemingly strange ideas or interpretations of day-to-day events which, while appearing odd to others, cannot be described as being held with delusional conviction. For example, Willy Wonka believes he has the perfect answer to taking the effort out of preparing a meal by having to shop and cook for it, or clear up afterwards: he has invented a type of chewing gum that tastes like a three-course dinner. Similarly, many of his other ideas, while highly idiosyncratic, do have a core of common sense, even brilliance, that cannot be disputed.

Those suffering from this disorder tend to speak in an unusual fashion. They are not incoherent, but often digressive. Willy Wonka takes a long time to explain about his newly invented sweets, going off on a tangent at every opportunity.

Prognosis

This disorder usually begins in early adulthood and has a chronic, though generally stable, course. Only a small percentage of sufferers go on to develop full-blown schizophrenia or another psychotic disorder.

Willy Wonka's condition is unlikely to improve, although if he were to continue to maintain a relationship with the Bucket family, he might learn to become more comfortable in social situations.

Treatment

As with most personality disorders, it is unlikely the sufferer will seek help. If they do, then psychotherapy or Cognitive Behaviour Therapy can be helpful in teaching the patient to interrupt distorted trains of thought.

No drugs have been designed to treat Schizotypal Personality Disorder specifically, but medication can be used for any accompanying symptoms, such as anxiety or depression.

HOW TO SPOT SOMEONE WITH A SCHIZOTYPAL PERSONALITY

Is there a Willy Wonka in your life? Are five or more of the following true of the person in question? Do they ...

have strange beliefs or 'supernatural' thoughts that influence how they behave? ☐

perceive things in an unusual or illusory way? ☐

seem paranoid? ☐

appear to speak in an odd way? ☐

behave, dress or present in an eccentric or peculiar fashion? ☐

appear to have no close friends or people they can confide in? ☐

seem very ill at ease socially, even amongst those they know well? ☐

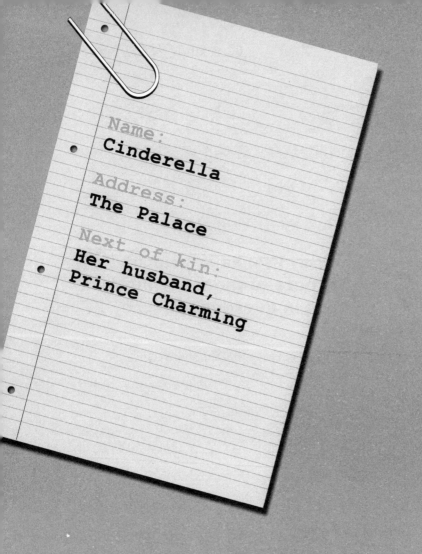

Name:
Cinderella

Address:
The Palace

Next of kin:
**Her husband,
Prince Charming**

'And they all
lived happily
ever after.'

Cinderella

Diagnosis
Approval addiction

Throughout her life Cinderella has pleased everyone but herself.
However, doing so, she has lost touch with her own emotions.

Physical presentation

Cinderella has a nervous demeanour. Her voice and facial expressions are childlike. She is well dressed, as befits her newly royal status, and is believed to have a penchant for unusual shoes – her only indulgence.

Diet

Little information is available on Cinderella's diet, although it is known that she was deprived of food when living with her stepmother and had to survive on scraps.

Family background

Cinderella's very early life was happily spent with her parents. After her mother's death, her father remarried a woman with two daughters. Although Cinderella was not accepted by her stepmother and stepsisters, she continued to live in this new family unit until her marriage.

Cinderella was born to affluent parents who enjoyed a good relationship. During her early years she felt loved and well cared for. This period of her life was uneventful, her upbringing was appropriately healthy and both parents played their roles well. The most significant and damaging period occurred after her mother's long illness and subsequent death. Everything then changed dramatically for Cinderella, and evidence suggests she felt deep grief, but was unable to express it as she didn't want to upset her father.

It would seem Cinderella's father found his wife's death difficult to talk about. Significantly, it was around this time that his daughter's people-pleasing tendencies began to surface. Although a child would be desperate to talk about his or her mother and make sense of her untimely death, Cinderella intuited this would be too painful for her father and so resisted expressing her feelings.

When her father remarried, Cinderella was initially positive. Burying her own feelings, she concentrated on the fact that this union would bring happiness to her father. His new wife, however, had no time for his daughter and treated her cruelly. She was banished to the servants' quarters and made to work long hours in the house.

Cinderella took her stepmother's rejection hard; but it was her father's reaction to this that perhaps caused the most serious damage. He refused to stand up to his new wife, allowing her instead to behave in an abusive manner towards his daughter.

Having been an only child, Cinderella was initially excited at the idea of having stepsisters. However, she became bitterly disappointed at discovering they were apt to be as cruel as their mother. The somewhat naïve young girl, having up to this point only experienced kindness, was shocked and bitterly upset by their behaviour. She internalised her feelings, however, believing that the treatment she received from her new family must have been in some way her fault.

The abuse Cinderella suffered at the hands of her stepmother and stepsisters may have led to a sense of low self-esteem and caused her to question her every action. It is likely she found it difficult to access her feelings and to be sure of what she wanted. Essentially, she had a poor sense of self and craved the approval of others.

Cinderella's life changed suddenly and significantly after

attending her first ball. Until this point in her life she had obeyed her stepmother's wishes and had not had any social contact outside the family. Rather than confronting her stepmother with the unfairness of the situation, Cinderella chose to go to the ball secretly.

It was while she was at the ball, that Cinderella met  the Prince, who was to become her husband. Although she was initially attracted to him, again she was unwilling to face her stepmother head on and instead left the ball suddenly without telling the Prince she was going.

The prince tracked her down, however, and asked her to be his wife. In accepting, Cinderella agreed to marry someone she had met only twice – he was the first man who'd paid her any attention – and the wedding was arranged for barely a week after their initial meeting. Cinderella perhaps confused love with a desire to be rescued from an unsatisfactory family life.

It is possible that Cinderella has been guilty of 'splitting' (seeing things either as all good or all bad) in casting her mother as 'always good' and her stepmother as 'always evil'. She has also created a drama triangle: she plays the role of the victim, casts her stepmother in the role of persecutor and the Prince in the role of rescuer. This is evidenced by the fact that she married a man she barely knew in order to escape her family home.

Approval addiction – the facts

Low self-esteem is at the root of approval addiction. Those who suffer from this disorder often had difficult or chaotic childhoods and, as a coping mechanism, learned to keep order by ensuring they pleased everyone. Of course, it's not possible to please everyone all the time. Hence, in trying to do so, approval addicts end up losing their sense of self. Approval addiction is also known as 'people pleasing' and is more common in women than in men.

Prognosis

If left unchecked, an approval addiction can become full-blown co-dependency (see Wendy p. 78 and Beauty p. 164), which is a much more difficult disorder to treat. However, if Cinderella commits to working with a supportive therapist and has the understanding of her husband, all indications are that she should be able to create and maintain fulfilling relationships. She needs to learn to set firm boundaries for herself and others.

Treatment

Cinderella would benefit from psychotherapy, through which she could explore issues from her childhood, work on her self-esteem and learn to give up her unhealthy addiction. Cinderella needs to confront the issues underlying her disorder, make peace with her past and move on. It might be appropriate for the Prince and Cinderella to attend some counselling sessions for couples, during which they might examine their relationship in a neutral setting.

Psychotherapy would help Cinderella learn to identify the things that are important to her. As she has grown up within an abusive environment, she'll do anything to keep the peace and needs to learn to listen to her inner voice, rather than looking outside for validation.

HOW TO SPOT AN APPROVAL ADDICT

Are you a typical Cinderella?

Do you find it difficult to say 'no' to the requests of friends or relatives? ☐

Do you find it difficult to make decisions without canvassing the opinions of others? ☐

Do you find yourself lying about things rather than saying how you really feel and risking a confrontation? ☐

Do you ever have a sense that you're unsure of what you really like? ☐

Do you worry endlessly about other people's opinion of you? ☐

Do you wish you could be more assertive? ☐

Do you feel powerless to change anything? ☐

Do you feel frightened at the idea of standing up for yourself? ☐

Do you wish you could be more like other people? ☐

Do you feel resentful that you seem to take more responsibility than colleagues or relatives? ☐

Does your behaviour enable the destructive behaviours of others? ☐

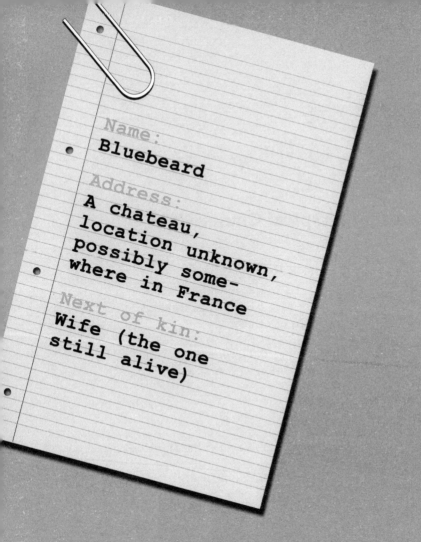

Name:
Bluebeard

Address:
A chateau, location unknown, possibly some- where in France

Next of kin:
Wife (the one still alive)

Bluebeard's superficial charm hides psychopathic tendencies.

Bluebeard

Diagnosis
Psychopathy
Bluebeard's callous disregard for others ends in serial murder.

Physical presentation
Bluebeard, despite a certain well-bred charm, is generally considered unattractive, possibly due to the disconcerting blue beard that hides the lower part of his face.

Diet
Nothing is known of his diet.

Family background
Nothing is known of Bluebeard's family of origin, apart from the fact he is a wealthy aristocrat. His unusual colouring possibly hints at more exotic antecedents.

Patient notes
Bluebeard is recently married to his fourth wife. The plight of the first three was initially shrouded in mystery; they seemed to have simply 'disappeared'.

Despite the lure of a beautiful house, considerable wealth and blue-blooded connections, local girls have avoided Bluebeard, understandably uneasy about the disappearance of his previous wives. It has therefore taken him some time to find his current spouse. The tenacity he displayed in searching for so long indicates a deep yearning for companionship, suggesting that loneliness and inadequacy may lurk beneath his superficially urbane and confident exterior.

Within the marriage, Bluebeard seems to be autocratic and controlling, limiting the areas of the house to which his wife is allowed access. Hence his fury, following his return home from a business trip, on finding telltale bloodstains on one of the keys to the chateau.

Further investigation revealed that his wife had stumbled upon the bodies of his dead wives hanging in a room she had been forbidden to enter. Her discovery of his horrific secret may well have tipped the balance within her previously even-tempered husband and triggered the murderous rage he then displayed.

Bluebeard clearly finds it difficult to control violent impulses when they come upon him, as a result of which his wife could now be in grave danger. Indeed, it is reported that she has locked herself in the tallest tower of the chateau while her husband rampages below, attempting to beat down the door and swearing he will kill her. Presented with such stark evidence that he was responsible for the deaths of his three previous wives, it seems reasonable to assume that he is more than capable of this.

Psychopathy – the facts

Psychopathy is a controversial diagnosis. Although it is currently not listed in the *Diagnostic and Statistical Manual of Mental Disorders*, many prominent experts are campaigning for its inclusion.

Unlike those suffering from a disorder such as schizophrenia, psychopaths can appear perfectly normal. Usually they seem intelligent, socially skilled, friendly and trust-worthy. They are, though, often described as mimicking emotions, rather than legitimately experiencing them.

It is easy to view a psychopath as a cold, ruthless individual incapable of experiencing normal human emotions. However, many psychopaths have described a lonely existence, in which they are desperate for friendship and suffer immeasurable pain due to their social failings and solitary lifestyle. One notorious psychopathic killer even reported that he 'killed for company' as he could not stand the intense loneliness he had endured.

Prognosis

Psychopaths rarely seek help for their condition. If they enter the mental health system, it is usually as a consequence of a court order.

Not all murderers are psychopaths and not all psychopaths are murderers. Many serial killers, though, do have a psychopathic disorder. Most murderers kill only once and for many different reasons. Serial killers – such as Bluebeard – develop a taste for murder and their passion for it escalates.

In Bluebeard's case, he has already murdered his three previous wives, and is now attempting to kill wife number four. There may also be other victims we are unaware of. Fitting the psychological template of a psychopath, he unfortunately is unlikely to see any improvement in his condition.

Treatment

It is notoriously difficult to treat someone with a psychopathic disorder. Behaviour therapy – through which the psychopathic elements of the patient's behaviour are treated as something that has been learned and therefore can be unlearned – may be offered. Cognitive Behaviour Therapy may also be tried, as may Psychodynamic Therapy, which uses a range of different therapeutic techniques. The patient may also be given medication, including antidepressants, benzodiazapines, psychostimulants and anticonvulsants.

HOW TO DIAGNOSE A PSYCHOPATH

Use this list of 'red flags' to see if you have correctly identified a psychopath like Bluebeard. Does the person in question ...

have a record of sexual promiscuity? ☐

show a callous disregard for the feelings of others? ☐

find it difficult to control their behaviour? ☐

have a grandiose sense of self-worth? ☐

lie pathologically? ☐

appear glib and superficially charming? ☐

show emotion in a shallow way? ☐

behave irresponsibly? ☐

have a number of short-term failed marital relationships? ☐

display a disregard for rules? ☐

blame others for everything that appears wrong with their life? ☐

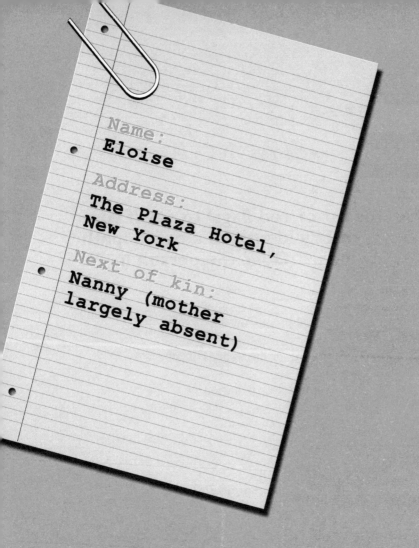

Name:
Eloise

Address:
**The Plaza Hotel,
New York**

Next of kin:
**Nanny (mother
largely absent)**

Eloise appears
spoilt and has
little regard
for others.

Eloise

Diagnosis
Conduct Disorder (mild) – childhood onset

Eloise seems to run wild and causes a good deal of trouble for all those around her.

Physical presentation
Eloise finds it difficult to sit still; she's always running around. Her mannerisms are flamboyant and dramatic.

Diet
Eloise eats oatmeal each day – she believes that anyone not doing so will dry up. Though she looks at the hotel menu every evening, she always orders the 'Planked Medallion of Beef Tenderloin with Fresh Vegetables Maison'.

Family background
Eloise lives at the Plaza Hotel, New York, with Nanny, her nurse. Her mother is not a stable figure in the child's life. It would appear her father is either estranged or deceased.

Patient notes
Eloise is largely cared for by her nanny. Her mother appears disinterested in her daughter's wellbeing and is rarely present at the Plaza or in her daughter's life.

Eloise has a series of superficial relationships. She has no peer-group friends, does not attend school and interacts only with those in her mother's employ and the staff at the Plaza Hotel. Eloise behaves in a bullying manner to those around her. While misbehaving and making unreasonable demands, she prevents staff at the Plaza from reprimanding her by constantly reminding them that her mother knows the owner.

Eloise has a pet turtle named Skiperdee. She braids his ears, puts him on a lead and makes him wear sneakers. While these may not be deliberate acts of cruelty, she is clearly showing a lack of empathy for the animal.

Eloise has committed a number of acts of vandalism. She scrawls her name on walls at the Plaza and regularly scuffs the skirting boards in the hallways. She also likes to pour water down the mail chute. She is possibly destructive with her toys, but this is difficult to ascertain for sure as she isn't always honest. In fact, she admits to enjoying making things up.

Eloise fails to follow any rules. She gatecrashes weddings, interferes with adults trying to do their jobs and deliberately sets out to cause chaos. This is evidenced by the way she spends hours riding in the hotel lift simply to confuse and annoy the bellboy. She also rings room service

 and orders ridiculous things, including on one occasion seven spoons and a raisin.

Eloise's most-used phrase is 'Charge it'. She has learned that, by picking up the phone, she can get whatever she wants. She places a high value on material things, often spending large amounts of time trying to work out how to manipulate adults into buying her presents.

Eloise sometimes acts up; she describes this as a temper fit. Usually, though, she finds less overt ways of communicating her displeasure. For example, she will refuse to listen to her tutor or repeat every word he says until he loses his temper. She also suffers from sleep disturbance, and almost certainly exploits this as a means of gaining attention.

It would appear that Nanny sometimes behaves in an inappropriate manner herself when in charge of Eloise, and is therefore not always the best role model. This is evidenced by her encouraging the child to watch fights on television, as well as drinking and smoking in front of her.

Conduct Disorder – the facts

Eloise's disorder is very mild, although perhaps worrying in one so young. Conduct Disorder is a persistent pattern of behaviour beginning in either childhood or adolescence. Those with the disorder engage in behaviours that violate the basic rights of others, transgressing age-appropriate societal norms or rules.

Sufferers may be aggressive or bullying; they may seek to intimidate those around them in a manipulative way (as Eloise does in her behaviour towards the staff at the Plaza) or they may be overtly violent. They are likely to destroy property or commit acts of vandalism, just as Eloise does in the hotel.

Those suffering from this disorder can be deceitful and may resort to theft, stealing from shops or people's homes, often with the threat of or actual violence. Sufferers tend to violate rules in general. They may fail to attend school, break parental curfews or even run away from home.

Prognosis

Eloise's condition is mild and the prognosis is good, providing the adults in her life ensure more stability. The child is very young and, with the proper support, she can learn a different set of coping behaviours so that maladaptive patterns can be broken.

Treatment

In this case family-based intervention would seem advisable. In the absence of Eloise's mother, her nanny could be taught techniques that would help curb the more excessive aspects of her young charge's behaviour, as well as diverting the child's copious energy into more constructive pastimes. It would be helpful for Eloise to attend school, especially one with a good deal of sport on the curriculum. Here she would be encouraged to develop appropriate relations with individuals in her peer group, as well as with figures in authority.

EXERCISE

HOW TO SPOT SOMEONE WITH CONDUCT DISORDER

Is there an Eloise in your life?
Has the person in question ...

bullied, threatened or intimidated others? ☐

behaved in a way that is cruel to either people or animals? ☐

deliberately destroyed the property of others? ☐

seriously violated rules? ☐

lied to obtain goods or favours? ☐

broken into houses or other buildings? ☐

stolen while confronting the victim? ☐

shoplifted? ☐

started a fire deliberately? ☐

run away from home overnight? ☐

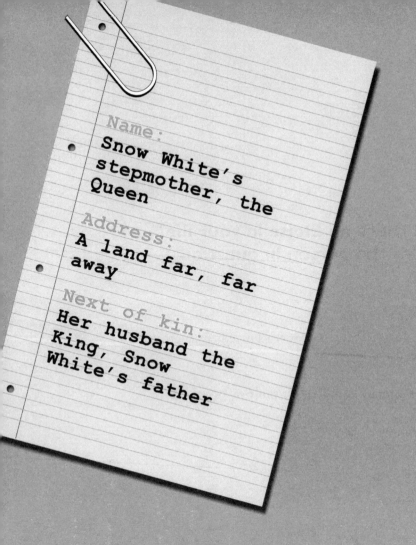

Name:
Snow White's
stepmother, the
Queen

Address:
A land far, far
away

Next of kin:
Her husband the
King, Snow
White's father

'Mirror, mirror
on the wall . . .'

Snow White's stepmother

Diagnosis

Borderline Personality Disorder (BPD) and Narcissistic Personality Disorder (NPD)

The Queen experiences severe problems in her personal relationships and in controlling her obsessive impulses.

Physical presentation

The Queen is very attractive and slightly preening in manner. This can give way to arrogance and aloofness.

Diet

The Queen appears to have a healthy diet. However BPD sufferers can behave compulsively in their attitude to food, eating either too much or too little.

Family background

Nothing is known about the Queen's background before her marriage to Snow White's father.

Patient notes

The Queen married the King after his first wife – Snow White's mother – died in childbirth. Initially the Queen's behaviour was appropriately maternal towards her stepdaughter. It was only once the girl reached maturity that the Queen found it impossible to maintain a stable relationship with her.

Snow White's stepmother shows obsessive tendencies concerning her appearance. She frequently looks at herself in the mirror and seems to require almost constant reassurance that her beauty is greater than that of any other woman. Her subconscious fear of rejection, even from the mirror when it indicates that she might have a rival in beauty, causes her to react with fury. She becomes paranoid and emotionally unstable as a result.

The Queen's relationship with Snow White broke down irretrievably once she became aware that Snow White's beauty was greater than her own. The Queen, with a tendency to see things in absolute terms, ordered the girl's murder.

Snow White's stepmother, rather than take responsibility for the deed herself, demanded that a huntsman should carry out the killing. Showing no regard for the man's feelings and no appreciation of the enormity of the deed she was proposing or the consequences for her husband and the country as a whole, she refused to listen to his reservations. When she learned, via the mirror, that the man had defied her and allowed Snow White to escape, the Queen raged explosively for days, only calming down once she had decided to murder the girl herself.

Dressed up as a peddler, carrying deadly wares with which to lure her stepdaughter to her death, the Queen seemed to play the role all too convincingly, perhaps because her sense of self is so unstable it's as easy to assume the persona of another as it is to be herself. The strength of her will and obsessive determination to destroy her hated rival are amply shown by her perseverance in trying three times to kill Snow White.

The Queen's mood stabilised once she believed Snow White was dead, although her total lack of remorse is striking. Her current equilibrium is unlikely to last, however, as sooner or later her mirror will reveal a new rival, especially as the years go by and age takes its inevitable toll on her beauty.

Borderline Personality Disorder – the facts

Borderline Personality Disorder is a painful condition for both the sufferers and those close to them. The disorder is essentially characterised by a pervasive pattern of unstable relationships and an intense fear of abandonment, separation or (as in the case of the Queen) rejection. BPD sufferers find it difficult to tolerate being alone and often react with impulsive behaviour, such as reckless driving, binge eating, substance abuse, overspending or excessive interest in sex.

Unlike those with Narcissistic Personality Disorder (see the Wizard of Oz, p. 100), they can feel empathy, but it is conditional on the other person being there to meet their needs on demand. If, like the Queen, a person suffers from both NPD and BPD, there is little chance they will be able to feel or show appropriate concern for another individual.

There are often instances of identity disturbance and dramatic changes of self-image. These can be characterised by changing values, goals, career paths, sexual identity and friends. For example, those with BPD might suddenly decide to move town and take up a new career, giving only a moment's notice to those around them.

Often individuals with BPD will have a distorted body image or place undue emphasis on their physical appearance. Seventy-five per cent of those diagnosed with this disorder are female.

Prognosis

The disorder is chronic, and long-term treatment is almost always needed, but with a lot of work on the part of the sufferer symptoms can be reduced. Once in therapy, BPD sufferers often begin to show some improvement during the first year of treatment. Follow-up studies show that, after ten years of ongoing treatment, around 50 per cent of patients no longer display a pattern of behaviour that meets the full criteria for Borderline Personality Disorder.

Treatment

Many sufferers find a marked improvement with techniques such as Cognitive Behaviour Therapy and Dialectical Behaviour Therapy (a type of psychosocial therapy designed specifically to treat BDP) used in conjunction with long-term pyschotherapy. Many doctors also advocate a mixture of antidepressant, anticonvulsant and antipsychotic drugs alongside therapy. It should be noted, though, that these only alleviate symptoms and modify behaviour, so should not be used in place of therapy.

HOW TO IDENTIFY SOMEONE WITH BDP

Is there someone you know who displays five or more of the following symptoms? Do they ...

feel a pervading sense of entitlement and therefore have an unreasonable expectation to be treated with particular respect? ☐

experience episodes of inappropriate rage? ☐

have a constant need to be admired? ☐

strive to avoid a feeling of abandonment, whether real or imagined? ☐

have an unstable or unrealistic sense of who they are or how they appear to others? ☐

fantasise obsessively about physical appearance, intelligence, success, power or the perfect relationship? ☐

demonstrate significant fluctuations in mood, frequently feeling anxious or irritable, or showing signs of dysphoria (see Eeyore p. 52)? ☐

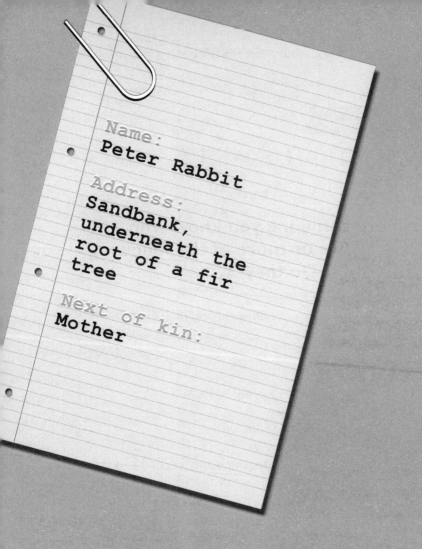

Name:
Peter Rabbit

Address:
Sandbank, underneath the root of a fir tree

Next of kin:
Mother

Peter Rabbit
shows no sign of
wishing to be a
good little bunny.

Peter Rabbit

Diagnosis

Oppositional Defiant Disorder (ODD)

Peter's defiant behaviour causes trouble for those around him and puts him in dangerous situations.

Physical presentation

Peter appears healthy and his eyes are bright. His stance is confident and slightly swaggering, and his clothes are dishevelled.

Diet

Peter has a vegetarian diet.

Family background

Peter lives in a secure family unit with his mother, Mrs Rabbit, and three sisters, Flopsy, Mopsy and Cotton-tail. His father is no longer alive. Mrs Rabbit is busy with four young children and is perhaps still struggling with her grief over the death of their father.

Patient notes

When Peter was very young his father was killed by Mr McGregor and put in a pie. This appears to have had a significant effect on the family. The three sisters behave in a compliant manner, knowing how hard their mother has to work to support them, Peter's stance, by contrast, is one of defiance. He deliberately breaks the rules, even though he is aware of why they exist. It's possible that he feels he's not getting enough of his mother's attention and that's why he acts up.

Peter defies not only his mother, but also other figures in authority, such as his uncle. Mrs Rabbit is very clear in the way she sets boundaries, and she allows her children an appropriate amount of freedom, so it is unlikely that Peter is reacting to being overly restricted in his movements. Peter's mother copes well with his defiance, however. She is patient with him and works hard to continually set the ground rules.

In particular, Peter has been expressly forbidden from entering Mr McGregor's garden – the site, after all, of his father's demise. However, Peter has completely ignored his mother's orders. He seems to know he can provoke her most by visiting the place that represents the greatest danger to the family. On one occasion, Peter decided to go there to steal food, even though his mother provides well for the family and he could have safely gone to pick blackberries with his sisters.

Despite almost being caught by Mr McGregor that first

time, Peter returned to the garden for a second foray, this time with his cousin Benjamin Bunny. The young rabbit's oppositional behaviour clearly hasn't abated, despite his being severely traumatised by his earlier experience, although he has admitted to feeling uncomfortable in the garden.

Oppositional Defiant Disorder – the facts

The existence of this disorder is usually apparent by the time a child is eight years old; it is unusual for it to be diagnosed after adolescence. ODD is characterised by a pattern of hostile, defiant or disobedient behaviour, towards parents or those in authority, lasting, crucially, at least six months. Children with this disorder tend to be resistant to compromise or negotiation and, while not usually physically aggressive, they can be verbally so. ODD is more common in children who've experienced disruption in their early care.

Prognosis

With the right care, sufferers of Oppositional Defiant Disorder can recover completely. However, another disorder is very likely to be present in a child with ODD. This could be AD/HD (see Tigger, p. 38), depression or anxiety. If this is the case, each disorder will need to be treated separately. ODD also shares many features with Conduct Disorder (see Eloise, p. 146) and a number of children with ODD go on to be diagnosed with this condition.

Treatment

Individual counselling can be effective in teaching a child how to manage anger issues. Family counselling can be useful too, teaching all the individual members of a family how to communicate more effectively with each other. It may be helpful in this case, enabling all the Rabbits to explore their feelings concerning the death of Peter's father. In addition, the parents of a child with Oppositional Defiant Disorder may benefit from being taught coping strategies and techniques for strengthening the parent–child relationship.

HOW TO IDENTIFY SOMEONE WHO IS OPPOSITIONALLY DEFIANT

Do you know a Peter Rabbit type? Do they often ...

enter into arguments with grown-ups? ☐

become easily irritated by the actions of others? ☐

fail to control their temper? ☐

seem prone to vindictive or spiteful behaviour? ☐

refuse to go along with rules set by adults? ☐

set out deliberately to antagonise others? ☐

place the blame on others for their own errors or wrongdoing? ☐

seem frequently bitter and angry? ☐

Name:
Beauty

Address:
The Beast's castle

Next of kin:
The Beast

'I was only
trying to
help . . .'

Beauty

Diagnosis
Co-dependency

Beauty's co-dependency creates difficulties in her relationships with other people, causing her to lose touch with her own feelings.

Physical presentation

Beauty's demeanour is cheerful. She appears very competent and with seemingly inexhaustible energy, as if nothing is too much trouble. Beauty is well dressed and clearly takes care over her appearance; she is always smiling.

Diet

Beauty eats a varied diet. Each evening the Beast insists on a five-course banquet for which she joins him. She appears to have no food-related issues, although sugar addiction is common in co-dependents and this could be true of Beauty; further investigation is required.

Family background

Beauty was a young child when her mother died. She was brought up by her father – who was often absent – along with her two sisters, with whom she has a difficult relationship.

Patient notes

Due to the lack of a mother and the frequent absences of her father, Beauty received inconsistent parenting as a child and her relationship with her family was difficult, especially following the collapse of her father's business. Beauty was distraught when poverty forced the family to move from their home in the town to an isolated farmhouse. This was a stressful time for them all. Indeed, it was then that Beauty's relationship with her sisters broke down and they began increasingly to abuse her.

Beauty was used to bowing to their selfish and demanding ways. But she is so compliant that even her father would take advantage of her on occasion, most notably when he was forced to 'sacrifice' her to the Beast in return for stealing a rose from his garden. He could have offered any of his three daughters, but it was Beauty who freely offered herself, and he readily accepted rather than give himself up.

Beauty's relationship with the Beast has a roller coaster quality to it and is troubled and traumatic. It could be said that, in moving to the castle to live with him, Beauty simply jumped from the frying pan into the fire. The Beast behaved abusively towards her from the outset, forcing her to take on domestic chores and constantly criticising her. She also had to cope with his terrifying rages.

Beauty grew so accustomed to such treatment that she was inordinately touched by even the smallest act of kindness, such as being permitted to leave the castle for the very first time to visit her sick father. This unselfish act on the part of the Beast seemed to trigger a transformation in him, however. On Beauty's return to the castle, she found a completely new man, entirely altered in appearance and temperament –

released, by the onset of empathy, from the 'curse' of living as an unfeeling 'beast'.

Now on an equal footing with the Beast as his wife, Beauty should feel an increase in confidence and self-worth that will make her more assertive. This does not seem to be the case, however, so ingrained is her tendency to put others before herself. Her sisters now impose themselves upon her uninvited, and Beauty feels unable to ask them to leave or to set boundaries around these visits.

She is torn as her husband doesn't like her sisters and believes they shouldn't be taking advantage of her in this way. This causes Beauty to be anxious and depressed, as she feels extremely uncomfortable about going against the wishes of others and, in this case, finds it impossible to please everyone.

Beauty's needs have gone unmet in all her significant relationships. The degree of responsibility she felt towards her father and now towards her husband is unhealthy, but she appears to be stuck emotionally and unable to change her behaviour.

Co-dependency – the facts

Co-dependents often grow up in dysfunctional families where they acquire maladaptive methods of coping, which later become a pattern in their adult relationships. While they tend to put the needs of others before their own, they shouldn't necessarily mistake their compulsive caretaking for compassion. They frequently form relationships with addicts or otherwise disordered individuals (see also Wendy, p. 78) and set about trying to 'fix' their partner. Co-dependents used to be referred to as 'enablers': they might 'enable' an alcoholic partner to continue drinking, for instance. Ironically, it can be when the 'disordered' partner gives up their dysfunctional behaviour that the co-dependent finds life unmanageable.

Co-dependents often mistake pity for love and stay in abusive relationships because they fear their partner wouldn't survive without them. They misguidedly perceive this as being unselfish. In the process, they compromise their own needs, feelings and integrity to avoid anger or rejection. It's also common for co-dependents to use caretaking as a means of controlling their partner.

The co-dependent may hold the underlying belief that if they fix their partner, he (or she) will be so overwhelmed with love and gratitude that he will never abandon them. Abandonment is the biggest fear of many co-dependents, who would rather stay in an unhealthy relationship than risk being alone, even if that would result in greater emotional stability in the long run.

Prognosis

Co-dependency is a learned behaviour, which – if she is to recover – Beauty needs to give up. In many cases this means leaving an unhealthy relationship. This is, however, exceptionally difficult for a co-dependent to do. Even if Beauty wishes to stay with the Beast, it would be wise for her temporarily to live apart from him. An inpatient stay at a treatment centre and/or attending a series of CoDA meetings (see 'Treatment', below) would be beneficial to her.

Co-dependent behaviour is learned in childhood and co-dependents have a high level of tolerance for unhealthy, abusive and inappropriate behaviour. Those who've grown up with chaos or abuse in their family feel familiar with it in their adult relationships, often finding healthy relationships somehow less comfortable. However, with the right treatment and support, co-dependents can go on to form healthy partnerships.

Treatment

CoDA (Co-dependents Anonymous) runs a 12-step programme based on the Alcoholics Anonymous model. There are CoDA meetings throughout the world, through which those wishing to recover can work at achieving more stable and emotionally fulfilling relationships.

A number of inpatient programmes are available to co-dependents. These tend to consist of group and individual therapy, including treatment designed to help the patient learn how to think and react in a healthier manner. No medication has been devised to treat co-dependency; however, if there is any accompanying anxiety or depression, appropriate drugs may be prescribed to deal with these issues.

HOW TO DIAGNOSE A CASE OF CO-DEPENDENCY

Could you be a co-dependent like Beauty?

Have you taken on the vast majority of practical responsibilities in your relationship? ☐

Do you feel that whatever you do it's not enough? However much you give your partner, do they still want more? ☐

Does your partner have abusive expectations? Do they demand constant attention, want you to spend all your free time with them and expect you to meet all their needs? ☐

Do you spend your time walking on eggshells? ☐

Did you grow up in a dysfunctional family? (You may have a higher level of tolerance to abuse or feel familiar living with this behaviour.) ☐

Do you find nice men/women boring? ☐

Do you feel responsible for – or guilty about – your partner's problems? ☐

Have you given up seeing certain friends because your partner doesn't approve of them? ☐

Do you spend more time thinking of how to 'fix' those around you than considering your own needs? ☐

171

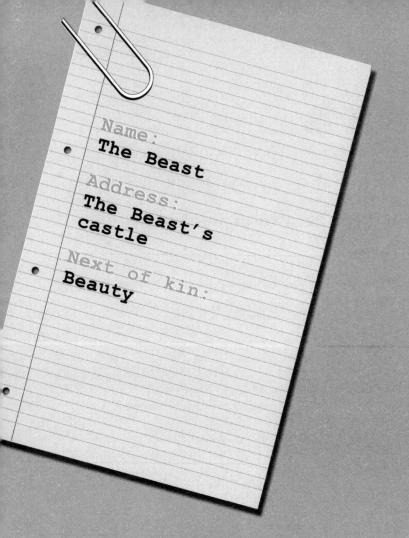

Name:
The Beast

Address:
The Beast's castle

Next of kin:
Beauty

The curse of living with the Beast can sometimes prove too much for those around him . . .

The Beast

Diagnosis

Ataque de Nervios

The shock of being cursed has caused the Beast to become irritable and aggressive, subject to uncontrollable rages.

Diet

There is nothing to suggest that the Beast's diet is unhealthy, although he does have a large appetite and insists on a five-course meal every evening.

Physical presentation

The Beast is half man, half animal. He walks on two legs, but is covered in fur and has hooves instead of human feet. His demeanour is tense and brooding, suggesting an inner rage that could easily erupt.

Family background

The Beast was born a prince and, by all accounts, his early life was contented and uneventful. All the members of his family were comfortable with their royal status and had no problems relating to one another.

The Beast had a happy childhood and grew up to take his rightful place in the royal family. However, following an encounter with an evil fairy (seemingly an occupational hazard for many a prince and princess), a curse was put on him and he was transformed, virtually overnight, into a totally different being – no longer a handsome, equable young man but a hideous, terrifying 'beast'.

It seems that, deeply depressed by this negative transformation, the Beast had changed completely in personality as well as appearance. His sunny nature and innate kindness were replaced by a black gloom, sometimes reducing him to tears, and an explosive temper. Since his transformation, he has behaved very badly towards those around him and has become arrogant, dismissive and exceptionally demanding.

Such is the extent of his brooding self-absorption that he has lost all ability to empathise with others and tends to overreact completely to minor events, becoming uncontrollably angry in an instant. Hence when Beauty's father picked a rose from the castle garden, but without first asking permission, the Beast rather than being mildly irritated was consumed with rage. He accused Beauty's father of theft and demanded that he either pay for it with his life or condemn one of his daughters to live, forever, at the castle.

In an act of self-sacrifice typical of her own disorder, Beauty (see p. 164) offered to come to the castle and now lives with the Beast, at his constant beck and call. He won't acknowledge the huge cost to Beauty of never seeing her family, nor try to make her feel at home to compensate for this loss. He treats her very badly, in turns ignoring her or raging at her. Although she does all she can to support him, he responds ungratefully and is forever criticising her, as though nothing she does is good enough for him. It is as though he has extended the curse that blights his life to encompass hers as well.

Ataque de Nervios – the facts

This disorder (literally, 'attack of nerves') is characterised by various symptoms, including uncontrollable shouting, crying, trembling, verbal or physical aggression and a sensa- tion of heat in the chest which rises to the head. The sufferer usually has a strong sense of being out of control. Some sufferers also experience seizure-like symptoms or faint, but this isn't always the case. Those with this disorder may also exhibit suicidal tendencies, although this doesn't appear to apply to the Beast.

The disorder frequently occurs as the result of a stressful event relating to the family, such as a death or divorce. In the Beast's case, it was almost certainly brought on by the shock of being cursed.

Prognosis

With appropriate loving support from Beauty, and professional help from a counsellor, there is no reason to presume that the Beast will not fully recover in due course.

Treatment

The Beast has suffered an enormous shock but his patterns of inappropriate behaviour have become ingrained, so it would be advisable for him to see a counsellor. Cognitive Behaviour Therapy might be useful in his case as it would help teach him how to control his rages. During these

sessions, he would be able to explore his anger towards the person who put the curse on him, as well as examining his feelings for Beauty. Looking to the future, as the treatment takes effect, the Beast would also be able to learn how to reassume his role as a prince and take up his royal duties once again.

HOW TO IDENTIFY A SUFFERER OF AN ATAQUE DE NERVIOS

Do you know someone who behaves like the Beast? Do most of the following apply?

Has the person in question experienced a stressful event relating to the family? ☐

Do they experience periods of uncontrollable shouting? ☐

Have there been bouts of crying? ☐

Have they experienced fainting spells or do they exhibit dissociative symptoms (see Tinker Bell, p. 84)? ☐

Do they return to their normal level of functioning after an aggressive episode? ☐

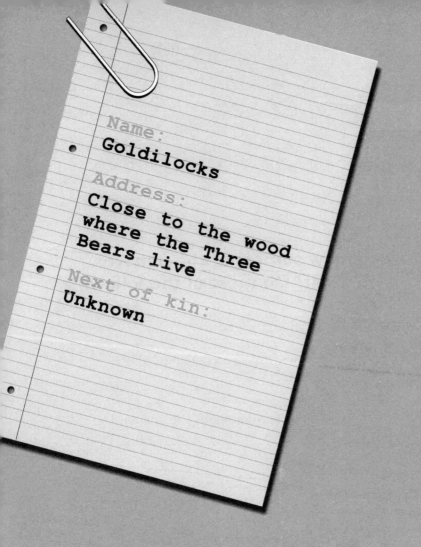

Name:
Goldilocks

Address:
Close to the wood
where the Three
Bears live

Next of kin:
Unknown

'I'll be sleeping
in your bed!'

Goldilocks

Diagnosis

Antisocial personality traits

Goldilocks behaves in a reckless and destructive way that violates the rights of others.

Physical presentation

Goldilocks appears physically healthy. Her most notable feature is her long, blonde hair, worn in ringlets and neatly tied with ribbons, which suggests that she is well cared for.

Diet

Other than a preference for porridge of a certain temperature, nothing else is known of her diet.

Family background

There is little information on Goldilocks's background, although evidence points to a family unit within a widespread rural community in which the younger members have considerable freedom to roam.

Patient notes

Goldilocks behaves in a selfish and reckless manner. She shows a disregard for the law and refuses to face the consequences of her actions. For example, she broke into the

secluded woodland home of a family of bears, ate their food
– although there is no evidence that she's denied sustenance
at home – broke their furniture and tried out their beds. In
doing so she was guilty of trespassing, theft and vandalism.

Such disregard for other people's property indicates that
Goldilocks lacks empathy. She treated the Three Bears'
house as if it were her own and when she broke a chair –
even one clearly designed for a child and therefore likely to
cause greater distress if it were damaged – she made no
attempt to repair it but simply moved on to wreak further
havoc in the upper floor of the house.

This insensitivity towards others is also evidenced by
the way she then tried out all the beds, a particularly gross
invasion of the Three Bears' privacy. Goldilocks will
not acknowledge quite how violating her actions were.
Moreover, not only was
the act of 'violation'
committed once in each
case but repeated, seemingly
out of a sense of perfectionism
that something should be neither too hot nor too cold,
neither too hard nor too soft, but 'just right'.

On finding that Baby Bear's bed met her criteria for
comfort, Goldilocks fell asleep in it, demonstrating a
remarkable ability to relax in circumstances that most
people would have found intensely stressful, as the Bears
could have returned at any minute. It also provides further

evidence of her lack of concern for the
family's feelings. When the Bears
finally appeared, she didn't
stay to explain her actions or
apologise for her behaviour.
Instead, rather than facing
their possible anger and any
punishment that might follow, she ran away.

Antisocial personality traits – the facts

Our personalities are made up of various traits, some of
which can be inappropriate and destructive. Individuals
with a certain number of maladaptive traits, which have
lasted for a lengthy period of time, may be diagnosed with
a personality disorder. Alternatively, a person may present
with a few such traits, as exemplified by Goldilocks. Hence,
like her, they might be impulsive, lacking in empathy and
showing disregard for their own safety and that of others.
As only limited information is available regarding her case,
it is not yet possible to diagnose her with full-blown
Antisocial Personality Disorder (see Captain Hook, p. 90).
However, if she were judged to have misbehaved in a
consistent way for an enduring period of time, rather than
over just one episode, and if her misbehaviour escalated
to include other traits such as violence, then it would be
likely she would be suffering from the disorder in its fully
developed form.

Prognosis

Goldilocks appears quite young. It is possible – with firm parental control and perhaps some individual counselling – that she will grow out of the type of behaviour shown and go on to live a fulfilling life.

Treatment

Family therapy may be useful in Goldilocks's case as through it the factors that have led her to show such disregard for others could be explored. One-to-one counselling would allow her, within a safe environment, to raise issues she may have or to deal with any underlying anger she may feel towards her family.

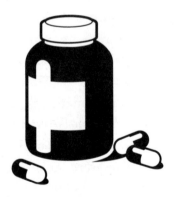

HOW TO SPOT SOMEONE WITH ANTISOCIAL TRAITS

Do you know someone who behaves like Goldilocks? Do they ...

appear to lack empathy? ☐

behave in an impulsive fashion? ☐

show a disregard for the property of others? ☐

have difficulty responding appropriately to figures in authority? ☐

have a strong sense of entitlement? ☐

appear to lack remorse? ☐

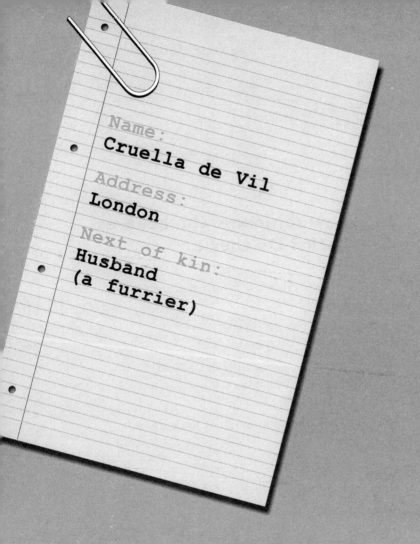

Name:
Cruella de Vil

Address:
London

Next of kin:
**Husband
(a furrier)**

Those puppies
would make a
fabulous coat . . .

Cruella de Vil

Diagnosis
Histrionic Personality Disorder (HPD)
Cruella's desire to be the centre of attention at all times is damaging to herself and those around her.

Physical presentation
Cruella de Vil uses her physical appearance to gain attention. Her hair, pulled back and parted down the middle, is black on one side and white on the other. She wears tight-fitting satin dresses and ropes of emeralds for quiet dinners at home and is rarely seen without a floor-length fur coat, sometimes even two at a time, as much for display as to keep herself warm.

Diet
Cruella has unusual tastes. She likes all her food – even the black ice cream she serves – to taste of pepper. She also appears to prefer her food to be unusually coloured, although serving dark purple soup, bright green fish and pale blue meat to dinner-party guests is probably more of an attention-seeking ploy on her part.

Family background
Cruella is the last of the de Vils. Her early life seems uneventful, although she was expelled from school for

drinking ink. She lives in London with her husband, but her ancestral home is Hell Hall in Suffolk.

Everything about Cruella de Vil is dramatic: the way she acts and speaks – direct and imperious, expecting everyone to comply with her demands; her provocative style of dress and her taste in interior decoration – ermine sheets and red marble walls. All of it screams for attention. Even Cruella's car – painted in black and white stripes to match her own colouring and with the loudest horn in the country – would appear to be another means of ensuring she is noticed.

Cruella is overly focused on her own comfort, regardless of how this might affect other people. She feels the cold, for instance, and demands that huge fires are lit, even though the heat is uncomfortable for others and leaves them panting. Her penchant for pepper-laced food, served to one and all, is similarly egocentric.

She feels no embarrassment in admitting that she married her husband only because he is a furrier (she claims to worship furs) and that she refused to take his name, demanding instead that he change his in order to preserve her family name, as she is the last of the line.

In her transactions with other people she also shows little empathy or, indeed, any sense of what is appropriate behaviour. For instance, her comment on first seeing the Dearlys' two Dalmatian dogs was that they would make a lovely fur coat – the perfect match for her black-and-white hair and zebra-striped car. Although Mrs Dearly tried to dismiss the remark as a joke, Cruella in making it had shown no regard for her feelings (or those of the two dogs). The remark also hints at the lengths to which Cruella will go to obtain another eye-catching garment; indeed, when the Dalmatian bitch gave birth to puppies, Cruella arranged for them to be stolen with a view to using their skins to make the longed-for coat.

Cruella lacks emotional depth and her relationships with fellow humans and even pets are entirely based on what she can gain from them. Her choice of husband was dictated by his profession; she befriended Mrs Dearly because of her dogs; and her own choice of pet is based on how it enhances her image, rather than from any affection for the animal. She has said she would drown her Persian cat if it weren't so valuable and admits to having drowned many of the cat's kittens in the past because they were not pure bred and therefore worthless.

Histrionic Personality Disorder – the facts

Those with Histrionic Personality Disorder feel extremely uncomfortable when they are not the centre of attention. They're often dramatic in their behaviour and speech and use their physical appearance to draw attention to themselves. To this end, sufferers of HPD will spend an excessive amount of time, energy and money on clothes and grooming, regardless of the consequences, financial or otherwise. In

Cruella de Vil's case, had she succeeded in her plan, she would have permanently deprived the Dearlys of their much-loved puppies simply so that she could have a new coat.

Prognosis

As with other personality disorders, those with HPD rarely commit to long-term therapy. This is either because they won't actually admit to having a problem and will have embarked on treatment only to appease their family or because they feel their chosen therapist isn't 'up to the job'. However, without therapy it is highly unlikely Cruella's condition will improve. At the very least, relationship counselling may be essential to save her marriage. After all, her husband is only too aware that she married for reasons other than love and may well become resentful of this and tire of her demanding behaviour.

Treatment

Personality disorders are perhaps the most difficult of all mental health conditions to treat. Those suffering from HPD take perceived criticism very badly and so find the therapeutic process particularly challenging. If Cruella were to accept any kind of treatment, Cognitive Behaviour Therapy and psychotherapy might help teach her how to step back and allow others to enjoy the limelight, lessening the need for her to resort to such attention-seeking, and ultimately destructive, strategies in future.

HOW TO IDENTIFY SOMEONE WITH HPD

Do you know someone who behaves like Cruella? Does the person in question display five or more of the following traits? Do they ...

act in a way that is exaggerated and theatrical? ☐

use their personal appearance to attract other people's attention? ☐

love being centre stage and are therefore uncomfortable when they are no longer in the limelight? ☐

behave in a manner that is inappropriately provocative or seductive? ☐

appear to fall easily under the spell of others? ☐

express emotion without actually appearing to experience the emotions so expressed? ☐

talk in a way that is both vague and obtuse? ☐

make more of personal relationships than is the case in reality? ☐

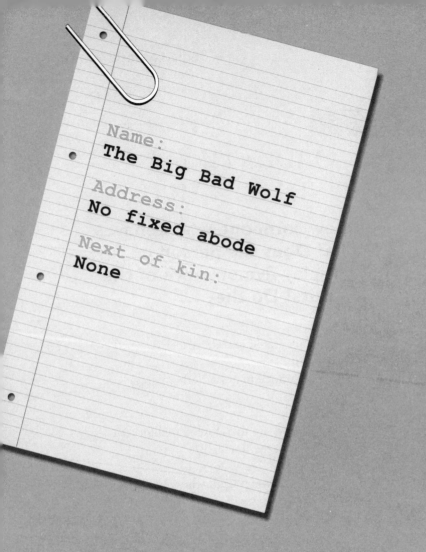

Name:
The Big Bad Wolf

Address:
No fixed abode

Next of kin:
None

'I'll huff and
I'll puff and I'll
blow your house
down!'

The Big Bad Wolf

Diagnosis
Psychopathy

The Big Bad Wolf's inability to follow rules or tolerate boredom, together with a total lack of empathy, leads to disastrous consequences.

Physical presentation

The Wolf's appearance seems to be of importance to him and he takes great care over how he looks. He is often seen wearing rather dandyish clothes and is preening and self-congratulatory in manner. There is also evidence he might have some respiratory condition as he tends to huff and puff.

Family background

There is no information regarding the Wolf's early life. However, as his condition is so extreme, it's highly likely that he experienced some sort of trauma or abuse during childhood.

Diet

The Wolf likes to catch and kill his own food.

Patient notes

The Big Bad Wolf has dropped out of society and leads a life of crime. He appears to have no family or peer-group relationships. His lifestyle is parasitic and he seems rootless and constantly on the move.

The Wolf is callous and shows a complete disregard for the feelings of others. He preys on the most vulnerable in society – the elderly and the very young – and appears quite unmoved by their plight. To date, he has murdered two of the Three Little Pigs and Red Riding Hood's grandmother, and it is likely that he has terrorised countless others. Indeed Red Riding Hood very nearly became his fourth (known) victim.

The Wolf met the little girl when she was on her way to take food to her grandmother's house. He gained her confidence by engaging her in conversation and asking lots of seemingly innocuous questions. Those with psychopathic tendencies often appear friendly and approachable; the Big Bad Wolf, for example, uses charm to insinuate himself into the lives of his victims. It is this ability to blend in that makes him so dangerous.

His grandiose sense of self-worth gives the Wolf a feeling of superiority over others. His need for stimulation and instant gratification, together with his inability to cope with boredom, have led him into dissolute ways. Add to these his lack of remorse and failure to accept responsibility for his own actions and it is easy to see how he has ended up in such trouble.

Like many psychopaths, the Wolf is work-shy and contemptuous of those who work hard, evidenced by the way he mocked the Little Pigs while they were endeavouring to build their own houses. When they mocked him in return, he grew angry and destructive, swearing he could actually blow down each house to get at its occupant.

It is interesting to note the lengths to which the Wolf is

prepared to go when trying to capture the last Little Pig. When pure violence fails, he turns on the charm and sets out to befriend his intended victim. In this way, he tried to manipulate both the last Little Pig and Red Riding Hood so that they would be lulled into a false sense of security and he could move in for the kill.

Intent upon luring his victim, the Wolf will resort to other forms of subterfuge as well. Having killed Red Riding Hood's grand-mother, he actually dressed up in the old woman's nightdress and cap and adopted her way of speaking in an attempt to ensnare the granddaughter – an attempt that very nearly succeeded if he hadn't opened his mouth to reveal a set of unusually large, ungrandmotherly teeth.

Psychopathy – the facts

The word 'psychopath' is often misused. Sometimes it is employed to describe those in the grip of psychosis, while on other occasions it is used as a loose description for a murderer. Of course, not everyone with psychopathic traits goes on to murder, but they do all lack empathy and have no feeling of remorse when their actions are hurtful to others.

It is important to stress that not all psychopaths present a physical risk to others. It is, however, common for those who enter a relationship with someone who has psychopathic traits to become emotionally damaged by the experience.

Psychopathy is a very difficult condition to treat, as often the sufferer will not admit – even to themselves – that there is a problem.

In the case of the Big Bad Wolf, his psychopathy is clearly dangerous and has led to murder. Most murderers kill only once and for many different reasons, whereas serial killers – such as the Wolf and Bluebeard (another psychopath, see p. 140) – will acquire a taste for murder and their passion for it will escalate. We know of three victims of the Wolf, but there may be many more. Note, too, the way the killings have progressed to two in one day, with the slaying of the Little Pigs. It is also common for a psychopath who murders to have a 'cooling off' period between killing sprees and – as is the case with the Wolf – to move on to a new hunting ground.

Prognosis

The Big Bad Wolf needs to be treated in a maximum-security unit. He poses an extreme danger both to himself and to others. Having murdered three times, it is unlikely he would ever be released.

Treatment

Since psychopathy is known to be virtually untreatable, it is highly unlikely the Wolf will ever recover from his condition. Nonetheless, he could undergo a course of therapy to help him to reconnect with his emotions and come to terms with what he has done. Cognitive Behaviour Therapy may be useful in teaching him to form healthier relationships with those he encounters in his new environment.

HOW NOT TO FALL VICTIM TO A PSYCHOPATH

Use this list to see if you may know a psychopath like the Big Bad Wolf. Does the person in question ...

lack empathy? ☐

have a very high opinion of themselves? ☐

lie continuously and without remorse? ☐

behave in a way that is calculating and manipulative? ☐

lack realistic long-term goals? ☐

behave impulsively and seem unable to 'apply the brakes' once roused? ☐

have a parasitic, possibly solitary lifestyle? ☐

break the law? ☐

refuse to accept responsibility for their actions? ☐

appear friendly and able to turn on the charm? ☐

seem unable to tolerate boredom? ☐

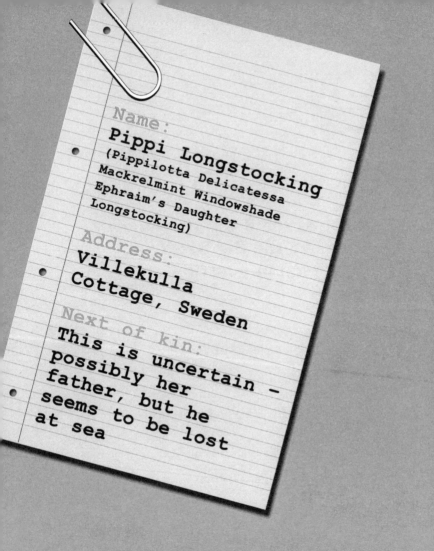

Name:
Pippi Longstocking
(Pippilotta Delicatessa
Mackrelmint Windowshade
Ephraim's Daughter
Longstocking)

Address:
**Villekulla
Cottage, Sweden**

Next of kin:
**This is uncertain -
possibly her
father, but he
seems to be lost
at sea**

Pippi Longstocking
behaves exactly as
she pleases.

Pippi Longstocking

Diagnosis

Personality Disorder Not Otherwise Specified

Pippi acts in a way that doesn't correspond with societal norms and can be disruptive.

Physical presentation

Pippi Longstocking appears physically healthy. Her teeth are well cared for, indicating that she doesn't forget to brush them. She wears her orange hair in neat pigtails, suggesting she takes care of that too. Her style of dress is eccentric; indeed she claims to make her own clothes. She also wears one brown and one black stocking and shoes that are twice as long as her feet. Pippi is exceptionally strong. She can, for example, easily lift a horse with just one hand.

Diet

Pippi cooks for herself, but does so in an unconventional fashion. She is fond of making pancakes, for example, but beats the batter with a bath brush.

Family background

Pippi Longstocking's mother died when Pippi was a baby. Captain Ephraim Longstocking, Pippi's father, disappeared on one of his sea voyages, although Pippi is determined that he is still alive and will come back for her one day.

Patient notes

Pippi Longstocking is nine years old and lives alone with her two pets – a monkey and a horse, which occupies the front porch of her house. She doesn't attend school and has no adult supervision at any time. Pippi can be self-absorbed and often behaves inappropriately in social situations. She is uncomfortable with figures in authority and has an odd way of thinking about ordinary things. Indeed her whole approach to life is unconventional.

Pippi holds entire conversations with herself. She might tell herself to go to bed, for example, but then refuse, so that she has to tell herself again more sharply. When, after arguing with herself for a while, she finally does make it to bed, she sleeps with her feet on the pillow and her head buried under the covers. Pippi often lies or makes up fantastic tales. For example, she might state that no one in the Belgian Congo ever speaks a true word and that people in Indo-China walk everywhere on their hands. When challenged she freely admits to telling untruths, however.

Pippi enjoys foraging for items such as ostrich feathers and rubber bands, but she can take this to extremes, forgetting to consider the feelings of other people. For instance, when she spotted a man sleeping on his lawn, she saw nothing wrong in picking him up and taking him home with her. She wanted to keep him in a rabbit hutch and feed him dandelions, as if he were a pet. It was only the intervention of her friends that stopped her taking him.

Pippi speaks to people in a superior manner and behaves as if her method of doing things is the only possible way.

Her problem with figures in authority causes her to miss out on things that would be beneficial to her. She would clearly benefit from formal education but to date she hasn't been allowed to attend school as she behaves too badly. Concerned neighbours contacted the authorities about Pippi on one occasion, complaining they were worried about her lack of adult supervision. The authorities duly intervened and found her a place in a children's home. When Pippi refused to go the police were called in. She spoke to the policeman in a facetious manner, refused to answer his questions sensibly and then defied capture.

There are countless other instances of her disruptive behaviour while in company. When invited to a smart tea party, for instance, Pippi picked up cakes with her toes and then dipped them into her tea. She sprinkled sugar all over her hostess's floor, stating that she found it fun to walk on the granules of sugar. She then fell into the largest cake and, claming it was now ruined, ate the entire thing.

Personality Disorder Not Otherwise Specified

This diagnosis is given to those who do not meet the full criteria for any specific personality disorder, but nonetheless exhibit a pervasive pattern of maladaptive personality traits. They may, for example, have a number of traits that derive from separate personality disorders. In Pippi's case she shares certain traits, such as her odd ideas and beliefs, with sufferers of Schizotypal Personality Disorder (see Willy Wonka, p. 126), although she doesn't meet the full criteria for this condition. She also has traits that are commonly found in individuals with Narcissistic Personality Disorder (see the Wizard of Oz, p. 100), such as her air of superiority and lack of empathy.

Prognosis

While it is unusual for someone as young as Pippi Longstocking to be diagnosed with a personality disorder, when one considers the facts it is obvious that this is exactly what she is suffering from. However considering her young age, and as long as she receives appropriate treatment, she is more likely to move on to lead a fulfilling life. But first of all she needs to be placed with suitable carers. As she is so against the idea of a children's home, foster parents should be found for Pippi. These should be kind and patient individuals, willing to teach her appropriate ways of coping. She should also attend a school where she is properly disciplined and where her unconventional upbringing is taken into account. Here she would be encouraged to form healthy peer-group relationships as well as learning how to accept instructions from individuals in authority.

Treatment

Psychotherapy would be an appropriate form of treatment for Pippi. In these sessions she would be able to explore any feelings of loss relating to the death of her mother and her father's disappearance. Having a safe environment within which to express such feelings and examine any related issues should prove very helpful to Pippi, whose view of the world has been shaped by her unusual familial circumstances and having to fend for herself.

HOW TO SPOT A PERSON WITH A NON-SPECIFIC PERSONALITY DISORDER

Do you know someone who is similar to Pippi? Do they ...

exhibit a pattern of behaviour that seems to deviate markedly from the norm? ☐

behave in a way that causes distress to themself or others? ☐

show emotion in a shallow way? ☐

not fit the criteria for any one personality disorder or type of mental illness? ☐

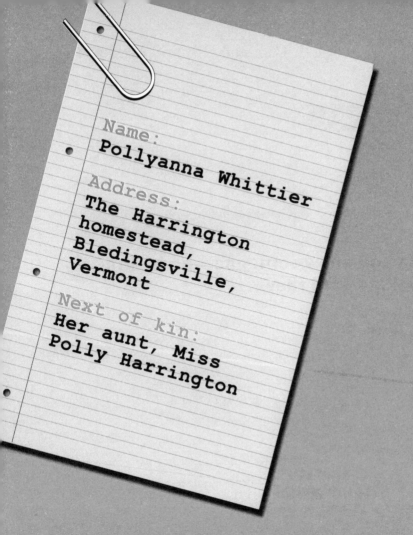

Name:
Pollyanna Whittier

Address:
The Harrington homestead, Bledingsville, Vermont

Next of kin:
Her aunt, Miss Polly Harrington

'When you're hunting for glad things, you sort of forget the other kind.'

Pollyanna

Diagnosis
Denial

Whatever happens to Pollyanna, she puts a positive spin on it.

Physical presentation

Pollyanna appears physically healthy; her hair is neatly plaited and her clothes are tidy. She isn't particularly positive about her personal appearance though, and she claims to dislike her freckles.

Diet

Generally, Pollyanna's diet is healthy. Her aunt is well off and has someone to cook for her. However, if Pollyanna doesn't arrive promptly for meals, she is given bread and milk and is excluded from the dining room.

Family background

Both Pollyanna's parents have died – her father only recently – leaving her an orphan at the age of eleven. She now lives with her aunt, Polly Harrington, who has never married and has no children of her own. Being the only surviving member of her family (with the exception of Pollyanna), her aunt has inherited the whole of the Harringtons' sizeable estate.

Pollyanna's aunt, stern and forbidding in manner, is perhaps not the most suitable guardian for the girl. She regards her late sister, Pollyanna's mother, as 'silly' (the latter having married a penniless young church minister of whom the family disapproved, rather than an older, wealthier suitor) and feels that she brought an 'unnecessary child' into the world. Miss Harrington has done little to make Pollyanna feel at home: she has allocated her niece a bedroom right at the top of the building, far removed from the rest of the household; she provides no comforts for the child and shuns any display of affection.

Outwardly, Pollyanna appears not to be upset by this. Indeed, she tries to find something good in every situation she encounters. She plays what she calls the 'glad game' – something her father thought up as a means of dealing with disappointment. For example, when she moved into the bare attic room assigned to her by her aunt, she decided to be glad about the absence of a mirror, as it meant she would not have to look at her freckles.

The glad game began several years ago when Pollyanna was very small. She had wanted a doll and so her father had approached the Ladies' Aid, a charitable group, asking if they could help. When they sent crutches, instead of a doll, Pollyanna was naturally disappointed. Her father then suggested the glad game. He told her that rather than dwelling on her unhappy feelings about not receiving a doll, she should instead be glad that she didn't in fact need the crutches.

Disappointment is inevitable in life. By teaching Pollyanna to ignore her feelings, her father was not preparing her for future disappointment, or indeed allowing her to develop a sense of perspective. Had he simply been supportive of his daughter over the doll incident, helping her to come to terms with her unhappiness rather than gloss over it, then Pollyanna might have been better equipped to deal with the difficulties she now faces at her aunt's house, rather than denying there is a problem.

Hence, rather than waiting to see how things might transpire, the newly orphaned Pollyanna decided before she arrived in Bledingsville that she was going to love living with her aunt. Even though Miss Harrington has subsequently proved to be cold and distant, as if she actively disliked the child, Pollyanna will not acknowledge this. Instead, she continues to state how happy she is and how well things are working out.

Miss Harrington made it clear from the outset that she

doesn't want Pollyanna to talk about her recently deceased father or even mention him in passing. This must be extremely traumatic for Pollyanna, who cannot, at this stage, have even begun to come to terms with her grief.

While there are, of course, many benefits of putting a positive spin on external events, by playing the 'glad game' Pollyanna is refusing to confront unpleasant realities and therefore cannot work towards changing them. Her aunt's harsh behaviour is inappropriate, particularly as Pollyanna has just lost her father. It is only very rarely that Pollyanna accepts her situation for what it is and cries about it.

Denial – the facts

Denial is a defence mechanism often used by those who find it too uncomfortable to confront painful truths. There are many different types of denial. On the one hand, it can be a defence mechanism resorted to by many of us on occasion when we refuse to face the consequences of something we have done and won't accept responsibility for our actions. 'It just happened!' is the all-too-common cry. In other cases, denial is more a habitual state of mind, as it is for Pollyanna with her misplaced optimism. In some families, for instance, an obvious case of alcohol, drug addiction or other maladaptive

behaviour exhibited by one
member may be denied
or minimised by the
rest of the family.
Alternatively, denial may
relate to a serious incident in a person's life. For example, if
someone has been attacked, they may acknowledge that the
assault happened, but deny its impact.

Pollyanna uses denial as an emotional shield. Although
Miss Harrington has made no attempt to welcome her
niece, displaying neither kindness nor affection, Pollyanna
simply behaves as if her aunt has been acting in an
appropriately supportive way. Having lost both her parents,
going to live with a relative who doesn't care for her is
simply too painful for Pollyanna to accept, so she denies the
stark reality of her situation.

Prognosis

Denial is often described as the defence mechanism of
an immature mind. Since Pollyanna hasn't yet reached
maturity, it is possible she will grow out of using denial as a
means of coping. While Pollyanna's optimism may be
damaging in her current situation, because she applies it so
indiscriminately, it could be helpful to her in the longer
term. Pessimistic people are more likely to suffer from
mental and physical illnesses than those who are more
positive in their outlook. However, Pollyanna will need

to learn to consider the facts more objectively in the future and be more realistic in her expectations, rather than being so blindly optimistic.

Treatment

Pollyanna has received very little support since the death of her father. Grief counselling, therefore, would be useful in helping her to come to terms with the loss of both parents. If possible, Pollyanna's aunt should attend some sessions with her niece, so that she can learn to deal with the child in a gentler, kinder manner.

Family therapy might also be an option. Both Pollyanna and her aunt could well benefit from this. Miss Harrington obviously has her own issues, as evidenced by an astonishing lack of empathy that may well stem from her childhood. In addition to which, suddenly having to take care of Pollyanna will have placed a huge emotional strain on her. Hence joint therapy might help teach them to co-exist in a manner that should prove more fulfilling for each of them.

HOW TO SPOT SOMEONE WHO IS IN DENIAL

Do you know someone who sees the world in the same way that Pollyanna does? Do they ...

seem to minimise their problems rather than addressing them? ☐

ignore issues that other people would worry about, such as hiding a bill rather than opening it? ☐

try to escape their problems in an unhealthy way – for example, using drugs, or alcohol? ☐

lie about how things are at home? For example, do they maintain that their marriage is very happy when it is obvious there are deep problems that need to be resolved? ☐

Final thoughts and acknowledgements

Mental illness is a real and painful problem. In the UK alone, one in six of us will be treated for depression at some point in our lives, and one in ten will suffer from a disabling anxiety disorder. Even more of us are likely to have friends, family members or partners who are sufferers. It is almost impossible to escape the effects of psychiatric disorders, which can be debilitating and frightening for both the sufferer and those around them.

My own life has been touched by the emotional disorders of family members, which has at times left me feeling helpless and alone. As well as the inherent difficulties in trying to support loved ones through difficult periods, there is also the frustration of coping with the stigma so often associated with psychiatric problems. Despite the fact that depression has taken over from back pain as one of the main causes of time off work, sadly it is still often treated dismissively or with suspicion.

These issues were at the forefront of my mind when I decided to write this book. My aim was to present mental illness in an accessible way which might help lessen the fear so often associated with emotional and psychological disorders.

Most self-help and psychology books are based on a single disorder and, by definition, are of interest principally to those suffering from that condition. By showing how many disorders can be applied to fictional characters we know and love, I hope this book has humanised mental illness in the real world and made its various manifestations perhaps easier to accept.

Thank you for reading, and thank you to the following people who have helped me to make this book possible:

My brilliant agent, Antony Topping, who has always been hugely supportive of me; I now find it difficult to contemplate writing even a shopping list without his input and approval. Jenny Heller, for being a great friend as well as a great editor. Kerenza Swift, who held my hand throughout the process and was always available to listen and advise. Kate Parker, for entering into the spirit of the book and being so great at editing my text. And a huge thank-you to Bob Vickers and Xtina Lamb, who made *Tigger on the Couch* look so lovely.

I'd also like to thank Zofia Falvey for all of her input in fact-checking and for brightening up my office every day.

Gareth Vincenti is a brilliant and inspirational psychiatrist and has been a huge help in reading my copy and making suggestions.

I'd also like to say thank you to Raffaella Barker, who is absolutely positively the most supportive and lovely friend anyone could hope to have and is always ready with tea and empathy at the precise moment both are sorely needed.

This book would have been doubly hard to write without the brilliant Rebecca Davis, who came over at the drop of a hat to entertain, feed and generally look after my children.

On that note I'd like to thank my children, Lucie, Tatti, Jack and Toby, for being lovely and also for making lots of suggestions for characters I might cover and for lending me their many books and not complaining when I didn't put them back.

There isn't nearly enough room here to mention everyone, but thank you to a huge list of friends for leaving me alone when I needed space to write and being there when I didn't and for sharing their personal experiences of emotional disorders.

Finally, I'd like to say thank you to Tim, who has been utterly supportive in giving me time to write, reading what I have written, offering advice and encouragement and keeping me supplied with vast amounts of chocolate, for all of which I am enormously grateful.

Resources

Further reading

A vast number of books are available, covering a huge range of disorders. The list here is designed as a starting point for those wishing to find out more about specific conditions.

Addictions

Alcoholics Anonymous – Big Book Special Edition – Including: New Personal Stories for the Year 2007 AA Services

Excessive Appetites: A Psychological View of Addictions Jim Orford

No Big Deal: A Guide to Recovery from Addictions John Coats

Sex, Drugs, Gambling, and Chocolate: A Workbook for Overcoming Addictions Arthur T. Horvath

AD/HD (Attention Deficit/ Hyperactivity Disorder)

ADHD: The Facts Mark Selikowitz

Taking Charge of ADHD: The Complete, Authoritative Guide for Parents A. Barkley Russell

12 Effective Ways to Help Your ADD/ ADHD Child: Drug-free Alternatives for Attention-deficit Disorders Laura J. Stevens

Understanding ADHD: A Parent's Guide to Attention Deficit Hyperactivity Disorder in Children Christopher Green and Kit Chee

Anxiety disorders

The Anxiety & Phobia Workbook Edmund J. Bourne

Change Your Brain, Change Your Life: The Breakthrough Program for Conquering Anxiety, Depression, Obsessiveness, Anger and Impulsiveness Daniel G. Amen

Depressed and Anxious: The Dialectical Behaviour Therapy Workbook for Overcoming Depression and Anxiety Thomas Marra

Freeing Your Child from Anxiety: Powerful, Practical Solutions to Overcome Your Child's Fears, Worries, and Phobias Tamar Chansky

Approval addiction

Approval Addiction: Overcoming Your Need to Please Everyone Joyce Meyer

I Need Your Love – Is That True?: How to Stop Seeking Love, Approval, and Appreciation and Start Finding Them Instead Byron Katie and Michael Katz

Borderline Personality Disorder

Borderline Personality Disorder Demystified: An Essential Guide to Understanding and Living with BPD Robert O. Friedel

Sometimes I Act Crazy: Living with Borderline Personality Disorder Jerold J. Kreisman and Harold Straus

Stop Walking on Eggshells: Coping When Someone You Care About Has Borderline Personality Disorder Paul T. Mason and Randi Kreger

Co-dependency

Codependent No More: How to Stop Controlling Others and Start Caring for Yourself Melody Beattie

Facing Codependence: What It Is, Where It Comes From, How It Sabotages Our Lives Pia Mellody

Understanding Co-dependency Sharon Wegscheider-Cruse and Joseph R. Cruse

Conduct Disorder

Banishing Bad Behaviour: Helping Parents Cope with a Child's Conduct Disorder (Parent, Adolescent & Child Training Skills) Martin Herbert

Conduct Disorder and Behavioural Parent Training: Research and Practice Dermot O'Reilly

Treating the Unmanageable Adolescent Neil I. Bernstein

Dysthymic Disorder

Dysthymia and the Spectrum of Chronic Depressions Hagop S. Akiskal and G. B. Cassano

When the Blues Won't Go Away: New Approaches to Dysthymic Disorder and Other Forms of Chronic Low-Grade Depression Hirschfiel

Intermittent Explosive Disorder

How to Deal with Emotionally Explosive People Albert J. Bernstein

Narcissism

All About Me: Loving a Narcissist Simon Crompton

Identifying and Understanding the Narcissistic Personality Elsa F. Ronningstam

Narcissism: Denial of the True Self Alexander Lowen

Why Is It Always About You? Sandy Hotchkiss

Oppositional Defiant Disorder

The Defiant Child: A Parent's Guide to Oppositional Defiant Disorder Douglas A. Riley

10 Days to a Less Defiant Child Jeff Bernstein

Your Defiant Child: Eight Steps to Better Behavior Russell A. Barkley

Personality disorders

Personality Disorders in Childhood and Adolescence Arthur Freeman and Mark A. Reinecke

Personality Disorders in Modern Life
Theodore Millon, Carrie M. Millon, Sarah Meagher and Seth Grossman

The Search for the Real Self: Unmasking the Personality Disorders of Our Age
James F. Masterson

Understanding Personality Disorders Duane Dobbert

Psychopathy

Handbook of Psychopathy Christopher J. Patrick

The Psychopath: Emotion and the Brain
James Blair, Derek Mitchell and Karina Blair

Without Conscience: The Disturbing World of the Psychopaths Among Us
Robert D. Hare

Shared Psychotic Disorder

Folie à Deux: An Experience of One-to-One Therapy Rosie Alexander

Support groups and organisations

Numerous international support groups and information-based services are available for individuals whose lives are affected by mental illness. The list below offers a starting point for those living in the UK wishing to obtain further information.

AD/HD (Attention Deficit/ Hyperactivity Disorder)

ADDISS (National Attention Deficit Disorder Information and Support Service)
Offers people-friendly information and resources about AD/HD
Tel: 020 8952 2800
Website: www.addiss.co.uk   Email: info@addiss.co.uk

ADHD UK Alliance
Working to raise awareness, influence policy and improve services for
children, parents, families and adults affected by AD/HD
Website: www.adhdalliance.org.uk   Email: info@adhdalliance.org.uk

Anxiety

Anxiety Care
Registered charity specialising in helping people recover from anxiety
disorders and to maintain that recovery
Tel: 020 8478 3400
Website: www.anxietycare.org.uk
Email: enquiries@anxietycare.org.uk

National Phobics Society
User-led organisation and the largest charity dealing with anxiety
disorders
Tel: 0870 122 2325
Wesbite: www.phobics-society.org.uk
Email: info@phobics-society.org.uk

Depression

Befrienders Worldwide with the Samaritans
Emotional support for people in distress
Tel: 08457 909 090 (UK local rate)
Website: www.befrienders.org   Email: jo@samaritans.org

Depression Alliance
Leading charity for people affected by depression
Tel: 0845 123 2320
Website: www.depressionalliance.org
Email: information@depressionalliance.org

Maytree Respite Centre
Sanctuary for the suicidal
Tel: 020 7263 7070
Website: www.maytree.org.uk   Email: maytree@maytree.org.uk

Eating disorders

Eating Disorders Association
UK-wide charity providing information, help and support for those
affected by eating disorders, particularly anorexia and bulimia nervosa
Tel: 0845 634 1414
Website: www.b-eat.co.uk/Home   Email: help@b-eat.co.uk

Mental health

Breathing Space
Information, advice and listening service available to callers in
Scotland
Tel: 0800 838 587
Website: www.breathingspacescotland.co.uk

First Steps to Freedom
Support for those with bipolar disorder, their friends and relatives
Tel: 0845 120 2916
Website: www.first-steps.org   Email: first.steps@btconnect.com

Making Space
Registered charity, providing practical help to people who suffer with
chizophrenia and those affected by serious and enduring mental illness
Tel: 01925 571680
Website: www.makingspace.co.uk

Mind
UK's leading mental health charity
Tel: 0845 766 0163
Website: www.mind.org.uk

Rethink
Rethink (previously known as the NSF – National Schizophrenia
Fellowship) is dedicated to improving the lives of anyone affected by
severe mental illness
Tel: 0208 974 6814
Website: www.rethink.org   Email: info@rethink.org

SANE
Comprehensive source of mental health support and guidance
Tel: 020 7375 1002
Website: www.sane.org.uk   Email: info@sane.org.uk

Schizophrenia Association of Great Britain
Help for those who need information and support, as a sufferer,
a relative, friend of a sufferer, or a carer or medical worker
Website: www.sagb.co.uk

Young Minds
National charity committed to improving the mental health of all
children and young people
Tel: 020 7336 8445
Website: www.youngminds.org.uk
Email: enquiries@youngminds.org.uk

Narcolepsy

Narcolepsy Association UK
Support and information about narcolepsy
Tel: 0845 450 0394
Website: www.narcolepsy.org.uk   E-mail: info@narcolepsy.org.uk

Personality disorders

Borderline UK
National user-led network of those who meet the criteria, or who have
been diagnosed with Borderline Personality Disorder
Website: www.borderlineuk.co.uk

Co-Dependents Anonymous (CoDA)
Informal self-help groups modelled on AA (Alcoholics Anonymous)
and using an adapted version of their Twelve Steps and Traditions as
a central part of its suggested programme of recovery
Website: www.coda-uk.org

National Personality Disorder Website
Information, resources and learning opportunities on personality disorders
Website: www.personalitydisorder.org.uk

Psychnet
Informative site covering all the major personality disorders
Website: www.psychnet-uk.com

Therapeutic services

British Association for Behavioural and Cognitive Psychotherapies (BABCP)
Multi-disciplinary interest group for people involved in the practice and theory of behavioural and cognitive psychotherapy
Tel: 01254 875277
Website: www.babcp.com

British Association for Counselling and Psychotherapy (BACP)
Search online for accredited counsellors and psychotherapists in the UK
Tel: 0161 797 4484
Website: www.bacp.co.uk

Relate
Long-established relationship counselling organisation
Website: www.relate.org.uk

Index